a letter from Gloria...

If there is one thing the Homecoming family of singers loves to do (other than sing), it is to sit around the table telling stories. Tales of the road, memories of growing up dirt poor in the south, great stories of tricks pulled on each other or on someone we all know are sure to be a part of every shared meal, whether it be a picnic behind the Gaither Studios, "in catering" when we're on the road, or on those rare occasions when a bunch of us are invited to one of our homes for a good old fashioned southern feast.

Over the years some of the singers have become famous for certain foods. Vestal Goodman often baked one of her legendary Coconut Cakes for someone and had it delivered to their bus when we were on tour. Lynda Randle has started a great tradition of making hot pancakes for every bus on the Homecoming Christmas tours and having her two "angels," Patience and Joy, deliver them steaming hot with a bottle of real maple syrup and butter. Then there's Wes Hampton's Carrot Cake and David Phelps' Five Flavor Cake that show up on our bus on special occasions. And there's nothing like Connie Hopper's Cornbread Dressing or Janet Paschal's Key Lime Pie.

When I have asked for the recipe for one of these delicacies, I have usually gotten something more like a "method" than a recipe – like: "Oh, I don't know exactly, but just heat some bacon grease in an iron skillet and stir in enough flour to..." and what follows are phrases like "until it feels right" or "when it's just about to thicken" or "'til it forms a ball when you drop a little in cold water that will clink if you tap it on the side of the cup." But in almost every case there is a story about who used to make this particular food and what happened the first time the dish was served.

We have found out a lot about each other in these conversations about food and family and memories. Over the years since these lovable people have come to be known as the Homecoming singers, I have come to know them maybe best because of the great conversations we've had over morning coffee on the bus, meals in catering in arenas all over the country, or in restaurants or truck stops late after concerts. It is at those times we have the courage and the time to "open up" about things that really matter like our kids, our parents, our dreams, our failures, our successes, and our faith. And always we end up laughing or crying together about how funny and how drop dead serious life can be. And as Bill likes to quote a line from George Younce, "We're part-time singers; we're full-time eaters!"

corn chowder

This is a family favorite because we would freeze corn from Daddy's garden and then use his corn for this soup. Frozen corn would be kept in the deep freeze in the basement and Mom would ask me to "bring a few bags up from the deep freeze." When making this, we would always make a double or triple batch. This is more than a soup...this is a *meal*. This soup, along with some biscuits, is very filling for those crisp fall evenings, and is great when reheated the next day.

Mom was never exact in her measurements. If it needed a little more cream, then she added it. She cooked to texture or taste, not to the specifics of a recipe. Her recipes are hard to pin down, but we have tried to document as many of her recipes as we could. (I believe she would have used more potatoes than what is listed in this recipe. She liked her soups hearty.) This soup is very easy, yet it tastes as if you worked over a hot stove for hours to get the flavor, especially when our Indiana corn is used.

1 onion, diced
¼ cup butter, plus additional butter for each bowl
¼ cup flour
1 cup cooked potatoes, diced
1 cup cooked ham, diced
1 bag frozen corn
2 (15.5 ounce) cans creamed corn
1 (10.5 ounce) can cream of mushroom soup
3 cups milk
¾ teaspoon salt
pepper to taste
chopped parsley

In a stockpot, sauté onion in butter until tender, being careful not to brown • Add flour, potatoes, ham, corn, mushroom soup, milk, salt and pepper to stockpot • Stir until combined • Heat to a boil • Place a pat of butter in the bottom of each bowl prior to filling with chowder • Garnish with fresh parsley

Mary Ann Gaither with her brothers, Bill and Danny

Mary Ann and Bill

MARY ANN GAITHER ADDISON

caramel apple pie

MARY ANN GAITHER ADDISON

My daughter Becky makes this delicious pie, but don't let the length of the recipe scare you. It's not difficult, and it is one of the best apple pies I have ever tasted. Usually when she makes this recipe she makes two; one is just not enough!

Gloria asked her to make this recipe several times for her parties when she had just graduated from college and was "catering"...if that's what you want to call it. Now it's a family favorite and a perfect recipe for the fall season.

pastry
2 ½ cups all-purpose flour
¼ cup sugar
1 teaspoon salt
1 stick butter
¼ cup vegetable oil
¼ water
1 egg

apple filling
6 cups granny smith apples, chopped and peeled
1 cup sugar
⅓ cup flour
2 teaspoons fresh lemon juice
1 ½ teaspoons cinnamon

caramel sauce
1 (8 ounce) package caramels - 28 count
½ cup half and half

topping
1 (8 ounce) package cream cheese
⅓ cup sugar
1 egg
⅓ cup walnuts (optional)

Preheat oven to 350 degrees • In a large bowl, combine flour, sugar and salt • Cut butter into flour mixture until fine crumbs form • In a small bowl, combine oil, egg, and water, beat until smooth and creamy • Slowly add wet mixture to dry mixture • Blend together until dough is smooth • Press dough into a 10 inch deep dish pie plate • In a large bowl, combine apples, sugar, flour, lemon juice and cinnamon and toss lightly • Spoon into crust • In a small saucepan combine caramels and half and half • Cook over low heat until smooth • Spoon caramel

Lela Gaither and Mary Ann

Becky with her Grandma, Lela Gaither

~⚯ continued ⚯~

mixture over apples • In a medium size saucepan, combine cream cheese, sugar and egg • Cook on low heat until melted and smooth • Spoon over caramel apple mixture • Sprinkle with nuts • Bake at 350 degrees for 35-40 minutes

what you have salad

When Michele and I got married, there wasn't a lot of money floating around. We were both working, but our careers were just starting, and we were on the low end of the pay scale, if you know what I mean. God has always blessed us and given us exactly what we needed even as our careers and growing family changed.

This particular time we were invited to a cookout and were asked to bring a side dish. We didn't have a lot in the fridge so we made use of what we had and came up with this salad. It was the first bowl empty at the party that night, and to this day people still request it. We just laugh.

1 head lettuce, rinsed and chopped and dried
1 green pepper, diced
2 cups carrots, shredded
2 cups frozen peas
1 package bacon bits or crumbled bacon
1 – 2 cups shredded cheddar cheese
1 ¼ cups mayonnaise

Cook bacon in a skillet until evenly browned, crumble and set aside • In a large glass bowl, place the chopped lettuce in a layer followed by layers of green peppers, shredded carrots, peas, crumbled bacon and shredded cheese • Spread the mayonnaise over the top of salad similar to icing a cake • Refrigerate until chilled

DOUG ANDERSON

Doug and his wife Michele on their wedding day

homemade caramel corn and mexican hot chocolate

Every winter we have a tradition at our house; when it snows, we go sledding and then come back inside to whip up caramel corn and hot chocolate. The girls, Isabel and Emma, look forward to the winter months to help Mom and Dad make up batches of these yummy treats. We have been making caramel corn for years now, and it has become our winter standard. The good and the bad part of this snack is that once you start eating it, YOU CAN'T STOP!

And what cold day wouldn't be perfect without hot chocolate? This is a recipe that we found that really spices it up. When I think of winter, the vision of the girls playing out in the snow and then marching back to the house with frozen fingers and toes comes right to mind. With red little faces, they climb onto the barstools and sip hot chocolate and eat caramel corn; only to thaw out and go back outside again.

DOUG ANDERSON

homemade caramel corn
½ cup unpopped popcorn (you can substitute with hulless popcorn)
1 cup butter
2 cups brown sugar
1 teaspoon salt
½ cup light corn syrup
1 teaspoon vanilla
½ teaspoon baking soda
1 to 2 cups nuts of your choice (optional)
1 package red hots® candy (optional)

Preheat oven to 250 degrees • Pop corn according to package directions • Transfer to a large bowl and combine with nuts and red hots • Divide between two glass 9 x 13 pans • In a 2 quart saucepan over medium heat, combine butter, brown sugar, salt and corn syrup • Stir occasionally until mixture comes to a boil • Lightly boil without stirring for 5 minutes • Remove from heat; stir in vanilla and baking soda • Slowly pour mixture over both pans of popcorn, stirring well • Bake at 250 degrees for 60 minutes, stirring every 15 minutes • Remove from oven and spread onto wax or parchment paper • Allow to cool completely before breaking apart • Store in an airtight container

The Anderson girls, Isabel and Emma

mexican hot chocolate
½ gallon milk
2 cups milk chocolate chips
2 teaspoons instant coffee
1 teaspoon cinnamon
1 can whipped cream

In large saucepan, bring milk almost to a boil • Add chocolate chips and stir until they are completely melted • Add remaining ingredients and stir well • Serve hot and top with whipped cream

Here is my wife's recipe for Karo Pecan Pie. I think it is the best I have ever tasted. This recipe actually belonged to Mim's mother, Mrs. Beulah Grantham. She went to be with the Lord in 1984 at the age of 92, but the story goes back to 1938 when the Blackwood Brothers were broadcasting on radio station WJDX in Jackson, MS. The Grantham's lived 35 miles southeast of Jackson in the little village at Weathersby which was actually named after Mrs. Grantham's mother. We were on the air each morning at 9:15, and Mrs. Grantham began listening to us each morning and got her daughter, Miriam (Mim), to listen. Mim wrote a letter to me requesting a song, and shortly after this we attended an all-day singing at a little Baptist Church in Weathersby. In the crowded little church, Mim was standing in the center aisle. I came up behind her wishing to start a conversation when I noticed she was holding a song book in her hand with her name written across the top. I recognized the name as that of the girl that had written me the letter. This gave me the opportunity I needed to start a conversation. Later she said, "Mama told me to invite the quartet to come by our house after the sing for pie and coffee." I eagerly accepted, and when we went by, I experienced my first taste of her Karo® Pecan Pie. Seven months later Mim and I were married.

This came from James Blackwood himself in 1997. He sang on many of the Homecoming videos before his death in 2002.

Miriam (Mim) and James Blackwood with little Jimmy

JAMES BLACKWOOD

mim's karo® pecan pie

1 cup sugar
2 tablespoons flour
2 eggs, slightly beaten
¾ cup light karo syrup
¼ cup milk or cream
1 teaspoon vanilla
1 cup broken pecans
2 tablespoons butter

Preheat oven to 375 degrees • In a large bowl mix sugar and flour, add eggs and butter • Add light karo syrup and milk; mix well • Add vanilla then stir in pecans. • Pour into unbaked pie shell and bake at 375 degrees until set (about 30 minutes) • Reduce heat to 350 degrees for approximately the last 20 minutes of baking time to prevent over browning ot crust and pecans

*About 20 minutes into baking you may want to use a pie crust protector, or tent the edges of the pie crust with aluminum foil to prevent the pie crust edges from burning.

nana's chocolate pie

Nothing holds a candle to my maternal grandmother's chocolate pie — at least in my eyes. As long as I can remember, Nana made her chocolate meringue pie for family get-togethers, including summer barbecues. Everyone knew she really made the pie because the recipe was "her Michael's" favorite. She made it with meringue, but I would always scrape off the meringue from my piece. So she started making two pies, one without meringue for me and one with meringue for everybody else. How great is that?

pie
1 (9 inch) baked pie shell
1 ¾ cups sugar
7 ½ tablespoons cocoa
4 tablespoons flour and 2 tablespoons cornstarch, or 6 tablespoons flour
2 cups whole milk
5 egg yolks (reserve whites for meringue)
2 tablespoons vanilla
2 tablespoons butter

meringue
5 egg whites, at room temperature
8 tablespoons sugar
¼ teaspoon cream of tartar

Preheat oven to 325 degrees • Thoroughly mix sugar, flour, cornstarch and cocoa in a medium bowl; set aside • In a medium saucepan, whisk the egg yolks and slowly add milk until combined • Slowly whisk in cocoa mixture to egg mixture • Add vanilla • Cook mixture over medium heat until it comes to a boil, stirring constantly • This will take 8-10 minutes • Boil the filling for one minute, then remove from heat • Stir butter into filling until melted and completely combined • Pour the mixture into baked pie shell

Combine egg whites, sugar and cream of tartar in a mixing bowl • Beat the mixture on high until stiff and glossy • Carefully spread the meringue over hot filling, making sure to seal the meringue to crust • Bake at 325 degrees for 15 minutes or until golden brown • Cool pie to room temperature before cutting

MICHAEL BOOTH

Ronnie and Michael are six years apart in age. When growing up, everything Ronnie did, Michael just knew he could do too, including riding a dirt bike. The Booth family lived on several acres of flat land, but an interstate was being constructed nearby, and the future entrances and exits of Interstate 75 became the boys' own personal dirt track. Ronnie was able to zoom up and down the hills easily, but Michael was small enough that he had difficulty mastering the steeper hills. He would ride up several feet and then roll back down.

One day, while wearing Ronnie's helmet, Michael pulled it off and threw it to the ground in frustration – breaking the shield. Finally, Ronnie decided to show Michael how it was done and even offered to ride Michael's smaller bike. That's when Ronnie discovered that Michael's bike didn't have the power he expected. He experienced the same fate as Michael; riding halfway up, stalling, and rolling back down the hill. Only this time, the bike flipped and Ronnie went one way and the bike went the other way. Of course, Michael was thrilled at this turn of events! Everything seemed to be just fine if his big brother couldn't get up the hill either! Michael's satisfaction didn't last long,

though. When he arrived back home, he found out that he had to do chores around the house in order to earn money to purchase a new helmet for Ronnie.

This was around the same time our family began making Broccoli Casserole. Ronnie, being the first born, was made to eat everything on his plate, but since Michael was the baby, our parents were more lenient with him. Today Ronnie will eat a brick if it had some sauce on it, but there are very few dishes that Michael likes. Until we were given this recipe, Michael refused to eat broccoli. Thank you, Aunt BooBoo (Beulah), for giving us this family recipe.

Ronnie and Michael Booth on the infamous dirt bikes that provided so many hours of entertainment when they were young.

The Booth Brothers today... Ronnie and Michael Booth, Jim Brady (seated)

broccoli casserole

2 (10 ounce) packages frozen
  broccoli, chopped
1 (10.5 ounce) can cream of
  mushroom soup
2 eggs, beaten
1 medium onion, grated
1 cup sharp cheddar cheese, grated
1 cup mayonnaise
1 (14 ounce) package herb seasoned
  dressing or stuffing
3 tablespoons butter

Preheat oven to 350 degrees • Grease
casserole dish • In a large saucepan,
cook broccoli according to package
directions • In a bowl, combine cream
of mushroom soup, beaten eggs, onion,
cheese and mayonnaise; mix well • Put
broccoli in 2 quart baking dish and
pour egg mixture over broccoli • Top
casserole with dressing or stuffing •
Add pats of butter • Bake at 350 degrees
for 35 minutes or until bubbly

best waffles

ANTHONY BURGER

Submitted by Anthony Burger several years ago.

I have two boys, A.J. is nine years old and Austin is six. A.J. is very quick when it comes to thinking. You can tell that Mark Lowry is his hero. Austin's big thing is every night before he goes to sleep, he says his prayers and immediately after he says "Amen" he will ask, "What are we having for breakfast?" One night he talked his mom into making "Green Eggs and Ham." Can you tell he likes to read? But this one particular night he requested waffles. So she got up early to fix a batch of waffles and as soon as they popped out of the toaster, the boys rushed downstairs. A.J. said, "Yea, waffles that's what I was thinking about." Austin was right behind him and said, "Yea, that's what I told mom I wanted last night." A.J. said, "Those are my waffles." "NO, those are my waffles!" Austin said. They got in this huge argument right there in the kitchen over who was going to get the first waffle. It was just like the Eggo® commercial on TV. So their mom broke up the fight and said, "Boys, quit fighting and behave. Now what would Jesus do in this situation? He would probably say, 'Let my brother have the first one, I can wait.'" A.J. quickly looked at his younger brother and said, "Austin, you be Jesus."

2 cups all-purpose flour
2 teaspoons baking powder
2 tablespoons sugar
1 teaspoon salt
2 cups milk
2 eggs
2 tablespoons vegetable oil
1 teaspoon vanilla

Spray waffle iron with non-stick cooking spray and preheat • In a large bowl, stir together flour, baking powder, sugar and salt • Add milk, eggs, oil and vanilla; mix well • Pour mix onto hot waffle iron • Cook until golden brown • Serve with butter and pure maple syrup or fresh fruit

LuAnn, AJ, Anthony, Austin and Lori

ANTHONY BURGER

ANTHONY BURGER

My favorite treat in the world is my mother's fried apricot pies. When I was really young—about 16 years old—I started traveling with the Kingsmen Quartet. I only made it home occasionally; but when I did, Mom would fix her delicious pies especially for me. Funny thing is, she would hide them, and I was the only one who knew where they were. The minute I walked into the house, I would look to see if she had hidden the pies. They were always waiting there just for me. When I would come out eating them—usually with a great big grin on my face—I would have uncles begging me to tell them where the pies were. They'd sometimes offer me up to a dollar just to disclose the secret location. But I would never ever divulge that information, and I would never let anybody share the pies. They were all mine! When I asked her to share her special recipe, the first thing she said was, "Recipe? You've got to be kidding! I don't have a recipe — I just throw it together!" So be warned that her recipe measurements are "approximate!"

mom's fried apricot pies

filling
1 package dried apricots
2 cups water
⅔ cup sugar

crust
3 cups flour
1 cup shortening
¼ cup ice water
½ cup butter, melted

In a saucepan, cook apricots with water over low heat for approximately 20 minutes • Mix in sugar • Cover and refrigerate overnight.

In a large bowl, add flour and shortening • Cut shortening into flour until fine crumbles form • Using your hands, work ice water into dough gradually • Knead dough until all water has been absorbed • On a floured surface, roll out dough to ¼ inch • Using a small or medium saucer, press out circles of dough • Spoon 1 heaping teaspoon chilled apricot filling unto center of each circle • Fold over and press edges together with fork • In a greased skillet on medium heat, fry each side of pastry for 5-6 minutes or until golden brown • Remove and brush with melted butter • makes 12 pies

Anthony

angel biscuits

My mother could really make bread. Maybe it was because my dad said that he would just as soon eat a wasp nest as a piece of light bread or toast! Of all her offerings, the family favorite was angel biscuits. They were served at the special family gatherings when we all met at the home place in Hartselle, Alabama. Naturally the recipe was shared with all those who enjoyed them. My folks are gone now, but my children now come to our home place, and as you might expect, they also look forward to Mother's angel biscuits.

Submitted by Bob Cain before his death in 2000.

5 cups unsifted all-purpose flour
1 teaspoon salt
¼ to ⅓ cup sugar
1 teaspoon baking soda
3 teaspoons baking powder
2 cups buttermilk
1 cup corn oil
1 package active dry yeast
2 tablespoons warm water
butter

Preheat oven to 400 degrees • Grease cookie sheet • Dissolve 1 package of yeast in 2 tablespoons warm water • In a large mixing bowl, mix buttermilk and corn oil and add to yeast mixture; mix well • Sift dry ingredients • Add to buttermilk mixture and stir • Cover with towel and let rise in warm place for 1 hour • Roll out dough on floured surface and pinch off a biscuit-size piece • Knead 5 or 6 times • Make a pocket for a pat of butter • Place onto prepared cookie sheet • Bake at 400 degrees for 15 minutes or until very lightly browned

Little Bob, Johnny, Jimmy and Loyde

BOB CAIN

mother's hot biscuits

My mother, Ethel Carter, is one of the best cooks in southern Ohio. Her specialty is Hot Biscuits. When the group (The Pfeifers) is leaving in the middle of the afternoon or late morning, Mom always fixes biscuits. Her famous saying is, "The journey is long before you, and biscuits will stay with you all day."

My mother is a great Christian example to me.

3 cups flour
½ cup shortening
4 rounded teaspoons baking powder
1 teaspoon salt
1 ½ cups buttermilk

Preheat oven to 475 degrees • Grease cookie sheet • In a mixing bowl combine flour, salt and baking powder • Cut shortening into flour mixture until pea size crumbs form • Add buttermilk and mix until dough forms • Roll out dough on level floured surface to one inch size thickness • Cut with biscuit cutter • Bake at 475 degrees for 10 to 12 minutes

MARY JANE CARTER

Ethel Carter with her daughter, Mary Jane

Mary Jane Carter of the Pfeifers

I didn't have a clue how to cook when I got married. (I'm smiling right now - those were the days!) I was seventeen when Phil and I married, and basically, the only thing I had done in my short lifetime was play the piano. This delicious recipe was something I came across in those early days that was easy for me to cook. It has since turned into a favorite for my entire family and now my girls are making it for their husbands-to-be and their families. I've never cooked it one time that adults and children alike didn't love this dish.

KIM COLLINGSWORTH

kim's chicken bundles

for chicken filling
3 medium to large boneless, skinless chicken breasts
1 (8 ounce) package cream cheese, softened
1 stick butter, melted
3 cans of crescent rolls (8 count each)

for crumb topping
1 cup seasoned bread crumbs
1 stick melted butter

for gravy
2 (10 ounce) cans cream of chicken soup
1 soup can water

In a stock pot, boil chicken until done • Remove from pot, cool and cut into bite size pieces • Preheat oven to 350 degrees • Lightly grease cookie sheet • In a bowl, combine chicken, cream cheese and one stick of melted butter; mix well • Spread on wide end of crescent roll then fold over, tucking the end point of crescent roll under so it doesn't come loose during baking • Mix remaining stick of melted butter with bread crumbs • Spoon one mound of bread crumbs on center of each bundle •
Bake at 350 degrees for 20 minutes or until crescent rolls are slightly golden brown

Kim and Phil

Meanwhile, in a sauce pan, add cream of chicken soup and one can of water • Heat

The Collingsworth family

∽ *continued* ∽

and serve gravy over top of
Chicken Bundles • Makes
24 rolls

low country boil

This recipe is a lot of fun to make. You can just toss in all of the ingredients and boil, then dump it on the table. Then everybody can just dig in like a bunch of pigs!

The father of our road manager, David Sikes, introduced us to this recipe. He is from Savannah, Georgia, and they have a fresh market there where he buys shrimp and crab legs.

He purchased the ingredients in Savannah, brought them to us, and served up this great meal. Of course, you can purchase everything you need at a store, which is what we do now when we make it, but buying the seafood from a fresh market makes it even better. Another good thing is that you can add or subtract ingredients from the recipe based on foods you enjoy.

5 pounds new potatoes
3 (16 ounce) packages cooked turkey sausage, cut into 1 inch pieces
8 ears fresh corn, husks and silks removed
2 pounds snow crab legs
4 pounds fresh shrimp
Old Bay® Seasoning to taste

Heat large pot of water over an outdoor cooker, or on medium to high heat stock pot indoors • Add Old Bay® Seasoning to taste and bring to a boil • Add potatoes and sausage • Cook for approximately 10 minutes • Add corn, crab and cook for another 5 minutes • When ingredients are almost cooked, add shrimp and cook for another 3-4 minutes • Drain water and pour the contents into an aluminum serving pan.

JASON CRABB

Jason cooking at home

chile relleno casserole

This recipe was given to me by a dear friend, Suzanne Niver, when I was in high school. Suzanne was a few years older than me and had siblings that were my friends. We all lived by the American River in Sacramento and spent many, many hours down there at a place we called "the log." It was a huge tree that had fallen and extended over the water.

The Nivers were dear people who loved to eat healthily and were avid gardeners. After high school I lost contact with Suzanne and her family. A few years back while I was performing in a local park, she and her sister showed up and we had a reunion!

Life is certainly a journey. I am seeing more and more how my long time friends are coming back full circle into my life. They are asking questions and searching. I just know God is up to something! (big smile)

I've always been fond of Mexican food so when Suzanne made this dish the very first time, I knew I needed to have this recipe! It has been one of my favorites for several years. My family and my friends are always happy to know it's on the menu!

Chile Relleno Casserole works as a breakfast or brunch dish, too. Enjoy!

LISA DAGGS

2 eggs
1 cup half and half
⅓ cup flour
4 (7 ounce) cans whole green chilies, drained
2 cups cheddar cheese, grated
2 cups monterey jack cheese, grated
1 (8 ounce) can tomato sauce or jar medium salsa

Preheat oven to 375 degrees • Lightly grease 9 x 13 baking dish • In a blender, mix eggs, half and half, and flour, set aside • Rinse chilies thoroughly and open up each chili to lay flat in baking dish • In the baking dish, layer chilies, cheeses and flour mixture until all ingredients are used • Pour salsa or tomato sauce over top • Bake at 375 degrees for 1 hour • Allow to cool slightly before serving

Lisa and Suzanne

I love to cook! So it was no wonder when I got married, the first thing I started doing was collecting recipes from everywhere and everyone I could.

We were living in Texas at the time, and Texas gals know how to cook! One of the first recipes I remember collecting was from my friend, Theta Hall, who lived in Fort Worth, Texas. She would often invite us for dinner, and one of the first meals she made for us was her Beef Brisket. It was so good; I thought I had died and gone to heaven! Whether we were having friends over or just having a family dinner, brisket became a favorite!

Because of my singing schedule, I often have had to be away from my family for days at a time. When I return I always try to make a home cooked meal. Of course, brisket is usually a first choice. On one occasion, I remember Tara coming home from school and excitedly declaring, "Momma's home," because she smelled the brisket when she opened the door. Every time she came home from college, I would have a brisket cooking.

This is a recipe that almost always makes an appearance on the table at our family gatherings. My husband,

Amos, is from a very large family. When we get together for a family reunion, we take turns cooking dinner for all 11 kids and their families. Now that's a large gathering! But Amos and I always had the perfect dish. You guessed it! Brisket! It is economical and easy, so you can see why it has become a tradition when we get together. If I am not there, Amos proudly boasts, "I will make dinner." That is how simple it is to prepare, and the leftovers are great for sandwiches. Just add a little BBQ sauce or mustard, and you're set!

Thanks Aunt Theta (as you are lovingly called by my daughter and granddaughters) for the recipe and for the memories it has made for our family. We love you and we love brisket!

Enjoy ya'll!

Theta and Sue

SUE DODGE

aunt theta's beef brisket

1 (3 to 5 pound) beef brisket
1 large onion, quartered
⅓ cup worcestershire sauce
⅓ cup soy sauce
⅓ cup liquid smoke
salt and pepper

Preheat oven to 250 degrees • Line a large baking pan with heavy duty aluminum foil (enough to wrap around beef brisket) • Place brisket on foil and top with quartered onion • Mix all liquid ingredients together and pour over meat • Lightly salt and generously pepper brisket • Cover with foil and seal tightly so that no steam or juice escapes • Bake brisket at 250 for 6-8 hours • Remove from oven and let it stand for a few minutes before slicing thinly on an angle against the grain

When I was growing up, the kitchen was the heart of our home. My mom was always cooking something delicious! From an early age, I remember sitting down together as a family for "supper." There was always plenty of good food, and we were always sharing it with good friends. Our kitchen was full of love and memories, so it is no surprise that when I got married 36 years ago, I wanted to carry on that tradition of good food and good company.

Amos and I started entertaining friends in our home right away. He was so proud of his new bride cook that he would often bring co-workers home for supper. One of the first big dinner parties I had was for the Speers. I think we had about 20 people in our home that night, and that was just the first of many dinner parties to come. Through the years, I've had the joy of having many wonderful Homecoming friends at my table: Bob and Jeanne Johnson, Lillie Knauls, Michael W. Smith, Russ Taff, the Easters and the entire Penrod family. (Yes, all 10 of them!)

My husband and I have been pastors for 30 years now, and our home has always been open to our congregation and our friends. Our kitchen has been the place to be!

Whether it's a small dinner party, a women's tea, a wedding shower, a baby shower, a staff dinner, a birthday party, a church open house or just an impromptu, good ol' fashioned family dinner, the food is always good, and there is plenty of it! I always keep my pantry and refrigerator freshly stocked, so that at a moment's notice I can whip up a meal or a delicious dessert.

This past winter we had a record snow fall in Washington DC, and we just happen to have the best sledding hill in the neighborhood. So...I invited our entire church staff over for a big country breakfast, sledding and hot chocolate! That morning, I cooked three dozen eggs, three pounds of sausage, two pounds of bacon, a huge skillet of gravy and about 50 biscuits! We had a blast, just sitting around the table eating, watching the kids sled down the hill and making precious memories. There is no better place to be than in a kitchen full of love!

I simply cannot name my favorite recipe. I love them all for different reasons and in different seasons, but here is just one of my family's favorites! It is a spring and summertime standard at my table. Enjoy!

Sue with her granddaughters
Madeline and Sydney

Amos and Sue Dodge

SUE DODGE

fresh strawberry cake

cake
1 white cake mix
1 small package strawberry gelatin
4 eggs
¾ cup salad oil
½ cup water
3 tablespoons all-purpose flour
½ cup fresh strawberries, chopped

icing
1 (16 ounce) box powdered sugar
½ cup strawberries, chopped
1 stick butter, softened

Preheat oven to 350 degrees • Grease
and flour 9 x 13 inch cake pan • In a
large bowl, mix all ingredients for
cake and pour into prepared cake pan •
Cook for 40-45 minutes • Cool
completely

For icing mix ingredients in a medium
mixing bowl until smooth and fluffy,
being careful not to over beat • Place
cake on platter and frost • Garnish with
fresh strawberries • Cover and store in
a cool place

hawaiian pie

Very early in the career of The Downings, we sang in Charles and Bess Kirby's church in Little Rock, AR. We became very good friends, and have sung in many churches where they have pastored all across the country. Bess and I are distant cousins, though we consider ourselves "close cousins."

Bess often had us in her home to share a wonderful meal or a dessert after a church service or concert. Many times we would share recipes. This Hawaiian Pie is one of my favorites and is full of coconut, pecans, bananas and sweetened whipped cream! I hope you enjoy this recipe as much as we have.

1 baked pie crust or graham cracker crust
2 bananas sliced
1 – 2 cups shredded coconut
1 cup pecan pieces
1 small can crushed pineapple, undrained
2 tablespoons flour
1 ½ cups sugar
whipped topping or real whipped cream

In a saucepan mix pineapple, flour, sugar and cook until thick, about 10 – 12 minutes • Remove from heat • Spread over pie crust • Layer bananas, coconut and pecans over pineapple mixture • Cover with whipped topping

ANN DOWNING

Ann and Paul at the Eastern Gate, 1973

mama's sausage rolls

One recipe I absolutely love is Mama's sausage rolls. Every year on Christmas Eve she makes them before she goes to bed and then bakes them on Christmas morning. Waking up to that ever-so-familiar and mouth-watering smell tells me that Christmas is here! Sometimes I forget about the presents and head straight for the sausage rolls...okay, that's not ENTIRELY true!

1 pound sausage
2 cups self-rising flour
1 (8 ounce) package cream cheese
1 stick butter or margarine

Preheat oven to 450 degrees • Grease cookie sheet • In a large bowl mix butter, cream cheese and flour • Roll out dough on level surface • Sprinkle raw sausage onto the dough covering the entire dough in a thin layer of sausage • Roll the dough from one end making one large roll • Slice roll in pinwheel shapes and place on a greased cookie sheet • Bake at 450 degrees for 12-15 minutes

MORGAN EASTER

Madison, Sheri and Jeff with Morgan

grandma's dressing

My grandma comes from a long line of great cooks. At 87, she still loves to make special dishes for her children, grand-children and great-grand-children. All of her sisters are also known for their great cooking. Many of them have cooked for special occasions like wedding rehearsal dinners, receptions, and parties for many of the folks in this little community we call home. It truly would be a disgrace to be a member of this family and be a failure in the kitchen.

My mom is also a great cook; however, for many years she attempted to create "Grandma's Dressing" since it was the favorite of all the kids and grandkids at our annual Christmas feast. Time and time again my mom tried, and time and time again, we reminded her that it was "almost as good" as Grandma's. It was probably because my grandma's recipe was a little of this and a pinch of that. After years of trying, my mama finally had achieved the honor of having her dressing deemed as good as Grandma's. Now, I guess it's my turn. It's a good thing that I'm as young as I am because I still have a ways to go. Here's the recipe for Grandma's Dressing with Mama's more accurate measurements for those cooks, like me, who need them.

SHERI EASTER

12 slices white bread, toasted and crumbled
2 cups baked cornbread, crumbled
1 large onion, chopped
5 eggs, well beaten
2 teaspoons rubbed sage
½ stick of margarine or butter, melted
1 ½ - 2 cups chicken or turkey broth

Preheat oven to 425 degrees • In a large bowl, combine bread, cornbread, onion, eggs, butter and sage; mix well • Add broth until mixture is the consistency of cornbread batter • Bake at 425 degrees for 20-30 minutes or until lightly browned

Grandma Lewis, affectionately known to Lewis Family fans as "Mom Lewis"

grandma's peanut butter cake

This recipe has been revised as it's been passed down. It was given to me by my sister-in-law, who changed it a bit for Biney, Michael's brother, and I kept it the same because Michael and Biney are so much alike in their tastes.

When Granny used to make this cake for Michael, she would put pecans on top. Michael doesn't like the pecans anymore because when he was a kid, he had his share of picking up pecans that had fallen on the ground from the tree in their back yard. So you'll not find pecans in this version!

When Michael's granny passed, his Aunt Linda made it for him. Michael was very close to his Aunt Linda, who passed away unexpectedly a few years ago. When I make this cake, Michael gets one of those dear, nostalgic smiles on his face, and it is clear whom he is remembering. To Michael, the very smell of Peanut Butter Cake brings back a flood of memories of two very special women in his life.

Marcie English

MICHAEL ENGLISH

cake
½ cup creamy peanut butter
½ cup butter softened
4 eggs
1 package yellow cake mix
⅔ cup water

icing
1 cup creamy peanut butter
½ cup butter, softened
4 cups powdered sugar
⅓ cup heavy cream or milk

Preheat oven to 325 degrees • Grease two 8 inch cake pans • In a large mixing bowl, combine butter and peanut butter; mix until creamy • Add eggs to butter mixture one at a time, mixing after each addition • Add cake mix alternately with water • Stir until just combined • Pour batter into prepared cake pans • Bake at 325 degrees for 25 minutes or until cake is golden brown on top and springs back when touched in the center.

In another bowl combine butter, peanut butter and cream until fluffy • Slowly add powdered sugar and mix well • Add enough cream or milk to make the icing a spreadable consistency • Cool cake completely before icing

Aunt Linda and Michael

Bill and Gloria Gaither in their kitchen

Jake Hess, Cliff Barrows, Bill Gaither and
Doug Oldham at The Cove

Foreground: Calvin and Joyce Newton
Behind: Deana Surles Warren,
Willie Wynn and Ben Speer

On left from front: Mitzy and Larnelle Harris, Russ
and Tori Taff, Marcie and Michael English, Wes and
Andrea Hampton, with Rory Rigdon (head of table)
On right from front: Dean and Kim Hopper,
Mark Lowry, Gloria and Bill Gaither, David and Lori
Phelps, Kevin Williams and Gordon Mote

The story is always better than the food.

Jake Hess Jr. with his wife, Judy (of The Martins), and their son Tripp (Jake Hess III)

The Goodmans: Howard, Rusty, Sam, Stella and Ruth stopped along the road for a homemade sandwich

Sharing conversations: Ben Isaacs, Sonya Isaacs Yeary, Gloria and Bill Gaither

strawberry ice cream

Like many Homecoming readers, I grew up in a church where we had an annual homecoming service with "dinner on the ground." (You must have been raised in church to get that phrase.) We often had church picnics, and nearly every summer my mom and dad and some of the other church families would take my brother, Bruce, and me camping. I don't mean KOA Camping, I mean build your own fire, haul the water and dig holes for...well, you get the picture. We would go to Ruidoso and Holy Ghost Canyon in the mountains of New Mexico.

One of my favorite memories is my mom making homemade ice cream for those picnics, dinners on the ground and camping trips. My mom mixed the ingredients, my brother, Bruce, would sit on top of the ice cream churn, and my dad would crank. It seemed like hours until the ice cream was ready, but it was worth the wait and tasted so much better than store bought ice cream.

Oddly, my dad, granddad and uncle owned an ice cream store where I grew up in Levelland, TX. It was great fun going there after school.

This is not a heart healthy recipe, but it sure is good.

LARRY FORD

1 package vanilla ice cream mix
2 tablespoons flour
¾ cup sugar
dash salt
4 eggs slightly beaten or egg substitute
1 (14 ounce) can sweetened condensed milk
2 cups milk
1 tablespoon vanilla
2 pints whipping cream
2 packages frozen strawberries or 3 cups fresh strawberries
whole milk

In a large bowl or food processor, mash or process strawberries (do not purée) • Set aside • In sauce pan, mix together ice cream mix, flour, sugar and salt • Add beaten eggs, sweetened condensed milk, 2 cups milk and vanilla • Cook over medium heat until mixture starts to bubble • Immediately remove from heat and cool slightly • Add 2 pints whipping cream and strawberries • Pour mixture into ice cream freezer • Finish filling freezer with whole milk to fill line • Follow instructions on the ice cream churn for churning

Larry with his mom and dad

benjy's best burgers

When summer heats up, there's no better place to be than outside cooking on the grill! My family and friends often come over for an evening cookout on the back porch. These burgers have become legendary, and it's all about mixing it up, keeping things creative and using good, lean ground beef. If you've got a craving for a taste of summer, grab your grilling gear and head outside for these hearty burgers. The guys especially love 'em!

burgers
16 slices bacon
1 yellow onion
2 cloves garlic
2 tablespoons dried basil
1 cup cracker crumbs
2 tablespoons worcestershire sauce
2 eggs
1 pound ground beef
4 hamburger buns, toasted

marinade
¼ cup olive oil
3 tablespoons lime juice
2 tablespoons teriyaki sauce
1 tablespoon balsamic vinegar
1 teaspoon each cilantro, garlic powder and onion powder
½ teaspoon cayenne pepper
½ teaspoon black pepper

Fry or microwave 16 slices of bacon: drain on paper towel and crumble 8 slices • set the other 8 slices of bacon aside • Prepare marinade by combining all ingredients listed above and set aside

Sauté onion and garlic and set aside • Once cooled, add the sautéed onion and garlic, crumbled bacon, basil, cracker crumbs, worcestershire and eggs to the ground beef • Mix well and form into four patties • Place patties in a glass

๛ continued ๛

dish and pour marinade over patties • Cover and allow to set in refrigerator for at least 30 minutes • Discard leftover marinade

When ready, lightly grease and preheat the grill • Cook patties for five to eight minutes on each side or until well done • Top with remaining bacon slices, fresh tomato, lettuce or condiments of your choice, and serve on hamburger buns

In Loving Memory...

Lela Gaither, mother of my late husband Dan Gaither, was a great cook. One of Dan's favorite dishes was her recipe called "Mock Steak" made with hamburger that included rich mushroom gravy. Lela's delicious mashed potatoes always accompanied it. Dan was a meat and potatoes kind of guy, and if I was to reach this man's heart, I knew I had to learn from his mother's masterful hand of cooking.

Lela's mashed potatoes called for a 5 pound bag, peeled, boiled and mashed. She would mix in one stick of butter, one can of evaporated milk and one pint size carton of half and half. On my first attempt to make Lela's delicious mashed potatoes, I mistakenly added a can of sweetened condensed milk instead of the canned evaporated milk she always used.

So, my mistake, coupled with Lela's own recipe turned out quite tasty and from then on, Dan always asked me to add a little sweet cream to the "taters." I once heard him bragging on me by saying, "She's a great cook, especially when she makes a mistake, it turns out great. It's just that she can't remember what she did differently." Dan and I truly enjoyed eating and cooking together. You can decide which mashed potato recipe to use, or perhaps find your preference somewhere in between. That covers the potato portion, now for the meat.

Vonnie Gaither Wright

Danny and his mother, Lela

DANNY GAITHER

mock steak

3 pounds hamburger
½ cup milk
¾ cup cracker crumbs
3 cans beefy mushroom soup
1 package dry onion soup mix

In a large bowl mix together hamburger, milk and cracker crumbs • Pat hamburger mixture in 9 x 13 glass pan • Cover and refrigerate overnight • Remove from refrigerator and cut into squares the following day • Preheat oven to 350 degrees • Flour hamburger mixture and brown in a skillet • return browned meat to 9 x 13 pan • Mix together three cans of beefy mushroom soup and one package of dry onion soup mix, stir together and spoon over mixture • Cover with aluminum toil and bake at 350 degrees for 30-40 minutes • Serve with mashed potatoes

caprese salad

Our grandson, Will, loved ordering caprese so much in restaurants, that I began making this Italian specialty at home. It is elegant, surprising and beautiful – so easily impressive with an Italian dinner. It's become a family favorite.

1 head fresh bibb lettuce
1 or 2 large fresh garden grown tomatoes
1 large purple or vidalia onion
1 log-shaped round of fresh mozzarella cheese
pure virgin cold pressed olive oil
balsamic vinegar
sprigs or leaves of fresh basil

Cover chilled salad plates with two or three bibb lettuce leaves • Place one large tomato slice on the bibb lettuce • Place one large thin onion slice on tomato • Place slice of fresh mozzarella cheese on onion slice • Drizzle olive oil and balsamic vinegar over salad and garnish with fresh basil sprigs • Refrigerate until ready to serve

GLORIA GAITHER

Gloria with her grandson, Will Jennings

no meat southern green beans

There is nothing as good as "good ole southern green beans" made with plenty of pork (ham, hocks, or bacon). But now that we are all trying to eliminate as much animal fat from our diets as possible, I came up with this heart-healthy recipe, and I promise no one will be disappointed. These green beans are great for babies and for grandparents alike. I love to put young red potatoes on top of the beans and cook them together. This dish says "summer garden" even in the dead of winter.

3 large family-size bags frozen cut or whole green beans
1 package frozen chopped onions (or three large vidalia onions, chopped)
⅓ cup cold pressed olive oil
2 teaspoons Seasoned Krazy Salt®
1 teaspoon seasoned pepper
8-10 leaves fresh basil, cut or chopped
baby red potatoes (optional)
¾ cup water

In a large pot, layer green beans, onions, seasoned salt and pepper • Add only enough water to pot to steam beans • Drizzle olive oil over the beans and clip basil leaves with kitchen scissors over top of last layer • Add washed baby red potatoes, if desired • Cook on high until water boils and beans start to cook • Reduce heat to medium low and cook for 1 hour • Gently stir as beans begin to get tender to mix flavors

GLORIA GAITHER

sour cream brussels sprouts

I have made this delicious dish for Thanksgiving and other special days. This recipe even converts people who think they don't like Brussels sprouts! The instructions say "serve immediately," but at our house that doesn't happen on Thanksgiving Day, because we first have to go around our gathered circle of family and friends until all, including the children, have shared what they are most thankful for since we last gathered like this, and someone from the oldest generation has asked God's blessing on this family, these friends and the food.

2 bags frozen brussels sprouts
1 medium onion, finely chopped
2 tablespoons butter
½ cup sour cream
salt and pepper to taste
seasoned sliced almonds (salad topping)

In a covered sauce pan add brussels sprouts, enough water to steam (½ cup or so), butter, onion, salt and pepper, and cook until tender • Remove from heat and drain off excess water • Gently fold in sour cream • Transfer to serving bowl and sprinkle with almonds • Serve immediately

GLORIA GAITHER

Gloria with her sister Evelyn, and their parents, Dorothy and Lee Sickal

gloria's death by chocolate

This is a recipe that shouldn't work, but it does and can be made in a flash. It is your private joke on the guests who think you've spent all day on this hot irresistible dessert. You can make it when you see them getting out of their car in your driveway! Serve it warm with ice cream.

1 box chocolate pudding mix (regular, not instant)
2 cups milk
1 chocolate fudge cake mix
1 (12 ounce) bag chocolate chips
1 small bag chopped pecans

Preheat oven to 350 degrees • Grease 8 x 8 or 9 x 9 cake pan • Prepare pudding mix with milk in saucepan and cook over medium heat as directed on package, stirring until pudding just begins to thicken • Add dry cake mix and stir quickly until smooth • Fold in chocolate chips and pecan pieces • Pour into 8 x 8 or 9 x 9 cake pan • Bake for 20 to 25 minutes at 350 degrees or until center feels firm and bouncy to the touch • Cut into squares and serve hot with vanilla bean ice cream and coffee or tea

GLORIA GAITHER

bill's favorite black bean soup

In the 'good ole days,' the things we remember our grandmothers making tasted great, but by today's nutritional standards had a lot of fats and seasonings we now know we should avoid. This version of a Cuban comfort food has no reasons to avoid and lots of reasons to serve often. Rich in fiber and protein, black beans are delicious and full of nutrition. This recipe, made with olive oil, chopped onions and salsa, has no animal fat or hydrogenated oils, yet is as delicious as you remember mama's to be.

I make a big pot of black beans, serve a delicious salad, make croissants or coffee-can wheat bread, and invite all the kids for dinner. I often make it on karate or music lesson night to help my daughters with their heavy schedules.

2 pounds dried black beans
2 envelopes onion soup mix
1 or 2 large vidalia onions, chopped or 1 (12 ounce) bag frozen chopped onions
1 teaspoon salt, add more to taste after cooking
3 tablespoons olive oil
1 teaspoon cajun seasoning or to taste
1 (16 ounce) jar medium salsa
rice, cooked

Wash beans in colander with very hot tap water until skins begin to pop open • Place beans and all other ingredients in a large soup pot • Add water to double the depth of beans • Cook on high until water boils; then turn to low and cook for at least 3-4 hours • Add more water, salt and Cajun seasoning if needed • When beans are tender, add salsa • Spoon a mound of hot cooked rice into large soup bowl, then fill bowl with black beans

GLORIA GAITHER

Gloria and Bill Gaither

lela gaither's barbeque meatballs

Isn't it delightful the way recipes gather ingredients and secrets as they are passed along like a snowball gathers layers of snow as it rolls down a hillside? These meatballs actually began with my mother. Then while I was making them, I discovered that if I dropped them in a kettle of boiling water to cook, the fat content would be greatly reduced, and I could always tell when they were cooked through because they would bob to the surface and float.

Then Bill's mom, the consummate country cook, finessed the recipe and worked her special magic on both the meatballs and the special sauce.

Now that she's gone, her granddaughter Becky makes them "just like Grandma did" and brings them to the family gatherings. They never last long, so no one has any idea what they would taste like warmed up for another day, but there's a lingering feeling that the longer they stayed in the sauce, the better they'd be!

meatballs
2 pounds ground beef
8 eggs
½ cup cracker crumbs
2 medium onions, chopped finely
1 package tomato-flavored dry cup of soup mix
sage to taste

sauce
1 (10.5 ounce) can onion soup
1 (10.5 ounce) can tomato soup
2 tablespoons cornstarch
2 cloves garlic, minced
¼ cup cider vinegar
3 tablespoons brown sugar
1 tablespoon worcestershire sauce
⅛ teaspoon tobasco sauce

In a large bowl, combine beef, eggs, cracker crumbs, onions, soup mix and sage; mix well • Form into small, firm balls • Drop into boiling water and cook until balls float to top • Remove and drain on paper towels • In a large bowl, combine onion soup, tomato soup, cornstarch, garlic vinegar, brown sugar and worcestershire sauce • Add meatballs to sauce • Mix well and simmer in a pot until sauce is thick and bubbly • Makes about 75 meatballs

Lela with Bill and Danny Gaither

GLORIA GAITHER

coffee can wheat bread

More and more I like making things myself to assure that my family isn't getting a bunch of chemicals, preservatives and additives to add to the already unavoidable toxins in our environment.

This incredible bread is easy to make, and I use organic unbleached and whole wheat flours and honey when I make it. It doesn't have to be kneaded and coaxed either. Just put the dough into a "greased" coffee can (two one-pound cans are my favorite size but you could use 1 two-pound can), grease the lid and put it on the can. Let the dough rise in a warm place until the lid pops off - no guessing - then bake. Be prepared though, this bread may not last long enough to make it to the table. Add a little real butter and a dribble of honey or sorghum and heaven can't be closer while you're still alive!

½ cup warm water
1 tablespoon sugar
1 package dry yeast
⅛ teaspoon ginger
2 tablespoons vegetable oil
2 tablespoons honey
1 (12 ounce) can evaporated milk
1 cup whole wheat flour
3 cups unbleached white flour

Preheat oven to 350 degrees • Grease well two 1 pound coffee cans, including plastic lids • In a large bowl, combine warm water, sugar, yeast and ginger • Let stand until bubbly • add vegetable oil, honey and evaporated milk to the yeast mixture and stir • Then add 1 cup flour at a time using electric mixer • Work in the final cup flour by hand • Drop batter in and seal cans with lids • Let rise in warm place until lid pops off • Bake at 350 degrees for 30-40 minutes or until golden brown • Let cool slightly before removing bread from cans • Serve hot and enjoy

GLORIA GAITHER

Gloria, Amy, Benjy, Suzanne and Bill

There is nothing more nostalgic or as traditional at Christmas as fruit cake or plum pudding. Trouble is, most people don't really like fruit cake. They say it's dry or it's too bitter with citrus. I kept experimenting with ingredients and various combinations from recipes until I came upon this incredibly moist, delicious and beautiful fruit cake. For starters, there isn't much cake – it's all fruit (no citrus), nuts and yummy goo. And, to top that off, it's soaked with an elixir that only makes the cakes grow more flavorful when kept wrapped in the refrigerator for two weeks or more. So I make fruit cakes early in December before things get too hectic, and when some dear friends drop by unexpectedly or I run into my beautician, Bill's barber or the UPS man (who are all old friends, too, by now), I have something to give that is from our own kitchen yet fit for the most elegant party.

Of course, I have to hide these cakes in the refrigerator behind the loaves of wheat bread, cartons of brown eggs and bags of fresh produce and grapes. If I don't, Bill finds them in the night and whittles away at them "just a sliver" at a time. I keep a couple where he can find them and bury the rest behind things.

nectar soaked fruit cake

ingredients
2 ½ cups flour
1 teaspoon baking soda
1 (28 ounce) jar mincemeat pie filling
2 eggs, lightly beaten
1 (15 ounce) can sweetened condensed milk
1 cup broken walnut or pecan pieces
1 cup candied red cherries
½ cup candied green cherries
½ cup candied pineapple chunks

nectar for fruitcakes
2 cups apricot nectar
¾ cups light corn syrup
¼ cup rum or brandy (if desired)

Preheat oven to 300 degrees • Grease and dust with flour one 9 inch tube pan, two regular sized bread pans or four small loaf pans

In a large bowl, combine eggs, mincemeat, sweetened condensed milk, fruit and nuts • Fold in dry ingredients • Divide into pans • Garnish tops of cake with half slices of candied pineapple, whole red and green candied cherries and halves of walnuts or pecans • Bake in slow oven at 300 degrees (2 hours for tube pan; about 1 hour for large bread pans, about 40 minutes for smaller

~ *continued* ~

loaf pans). Check centers with a toothpick for doneness • When toothpick comes out clean, remove from oven

While cakes are baking, heat corn syrup and apricot nectar in a sauce pan until just ready to boil • Add rum or brandy and turn off heat and cover • When cakes are done, using a meat fork, poke holes in cakes and spoon nectar over cakes allowing the liquid to soak into cakes • Continue until cakes have absorbed liquid and surfaces are glazed • Let cakes cool in pans • When cool, turn each cake upside-down on heavy plastic wrap; wrap and seal • Wrap again in foil and store in refrigerator for up to three weeks

My mother was a busy woman (pastor's wife, writer, youth leader, artist and mother), yet it was important for her to create and maintain a warm and welcoming home. Her molasses cookies and others are still sure to bring back to me dear memories of her and our home. She made these cookies for us at home and also often gave them away as comfort to the grieving or in celebration of a new baby or special occasion.

These molasses cookies were given for harvest time or Christmas. Gold boxes layered with cookies between sheets of waxed paper were tied with gingham ribbon or lace and given as a hostess gift or a welcome-to-the-neighborhood present. Sometimes she would put these chewy wonders in a container tied with a fabric strip and give them to a new parishioner or neighbor with a "keep the container" note.

The taste of molasses of any kind and sorghum in particular reminds me of my dad, who loved sorghum and put it on everything from wheat toast to cottage cheese. To this day I keep a squeeze bottle of sorghum in the cupboard to put on warm biscuits,

homemade wheat bread or bran muffins.

Tastes are a link to those we love as surely as are songs, phrases, sights and photo albums. My sister and I are orphans now, but these heart warming tastes and smells are an embrace from parents now gone that we pass on with real hugs to the children of our children.

GLORIA GAITHER

Gloria's mom, Dorothy Sickal, with grandchildren, Suzanne, Lisa Baylor, Benjy and Amy at Camp Meeting

mother's soft molasses cookies

1 cup natural dark molasses
1 cup packed brown sugar
1 cup melted butter
4 cups flour (just a bit less)
1 teaspoon each of the following:
  baking soda, allspice, cinnamon,
  mace, cloves, nutmeg, ginger and salt
1 cup chopped pecans or english
  walnuts

Preheat oven to 350 degrees • Grease cookie sheet • Mix molasses, brown sugar, and melted butter in a mixing bowl • Slowly add just under 4 cups flour and sprinkle in spices; mix well • Fold in chopped nuts • Divide into three portions and roll into logs about 2 inches in diameter • Wrap each log in plastic wrap and chill for at least one hour • Slice dough in ½ inch thick sections and bake at 350 degrees for 10 minutes, being careful not to over bake • Cool and store in sealed plastic container between layers of wax paper • These cookies are incredible with tea, milk or good coffee

You may keep this dough for a few days in the refrigerator or freeze it up to 6 weeks. Just be sure to double-wrap dough in plastic wrap. When you are ready to bake, simply let the dough defrost in the refrigerator.

red raspberry cake

This recipe was given to me by my mother and is the number one favorite around the Gaither home. It has been served for nearly every birthday since our kids were little and is now a favorite of our grandchildren.

There's something decidedly celebratory about a combination of pink and red—and with raspberry flavor to boot! One of the earliest memories of this Gaither family favorite, at least for our eldest daughter, Suzanne, is a birthday party to which almost half of her second-grade class was invited. With Suzanne's birthday in December and very close to Christmas, we wanted to make sure that it wasn't overlooked in all the bustle of the holidays.

I love to be festive and had created a full party décor of pink and red, including gifts wrapped in the same duet of rosy colors. Nothing else would do but that the cake should match! And who doesn't love raspberries in December? Or in mid-summer, years later, as when Suzanne chose the recipe for her wedding cake! Of course, everyone who nurses a sweet tooth has memories of a cake recipe that is simply "to die for," but here's one that offers a bonus—fresh raspberry taste in both the cake and the icing!

cake
1 package white cake mix
1 (10 ounce) package frozen red raspberries
3 level tablespoons flour
1 small package of raspberry gelatin (not sugar free)
½ cup cold water
1 cup vegetable oil
4 eggs

icing
1 stick butter or 100% corn oil margarine
1 pound powdered sugar (3 ½ to 4 cups)
½ remaining package thawed red raspberries

Preheat oven to 350 degrees • Grease three 8 inch or two 9 inch cake pans • In large bowl mix dry ingredients • To dry ingredients alternately add oil, water and eggs (adding eggs one at a time) • Do not over beat • Break up ½ package of frozen raspberries (saving other ½ for icing) and fold into batter • Bake at 350 degrees for 30 to 35 minutes or until the center springs back when touched • Be sure cake is completely cool or even refrigerate until cold before icing

icing glaze: Mix all ingredients in a bowl and whip with mixer until well blended

spreadable icing: Add additional powdered sugar until desired consistency.

Gloria's daughter-in-law Melody, with little Liam

Gloria's mother, Dorothy Sickal

clela's oatmeal cookies

This recipe came from a dear lady in my parents' church in Burlington, Michigan. It was the first and best cookie I ever learned to make.

2 cups flour
1 teaspoon salt
1 teaspoon baking powder
1 teaspoon baking soda
1 cup brown sugar
1 cup white sugar
1 cup soft shortening
2 eggs
1 teaspoon vanilla
3 cups rolled oats
1 cup raisins (optional)
1 (4 ounces) individual serving cup of applesauce or 1 large jar of junior baby food applesauce

Preheat oven to 375 degrees • Grease cookie sheet • In a large mixing bowl, combine shortening, sugar, eggs and vanilla • In another bowl, mix flour, salt, baking soda, and baking powder • Add dry mixture slowly to egg, sugar and shortening mixture • Mix well • Add applesauce and one cup raisins • With heavy spoon or by hand, mix in three cups oatmeal until well blended • Drop balls of cookie dough onto greased cookie sheet • Bake for 10 minutes at 375 degrees • Cool and store in sealed plastic container to keep moist and chewy

Clela teaching Sunday school at our church in Burlington

GLORIA GAITHER

The only time of the whole year I make chipped dried beef gravy and biscuits is Christmas morning. The whole family crowds around our big oak table by the kitchen fire (which Bill keeps burning all night Christmas Eve), and there is much happy conversation and story-telling. With the gravy and biscuits I usually serve fresh fruit (berries, melon, mandarin oranges, bananas) in glasses I've chilled in the freezer and a big plate of scrambled eggs sprinkled with grated cheddar cheese.

When the children were home, this breakfast followed the reading of the Christmas story from Luke 2 and opening of gifts, but now that they open Christmas presents in their own homes early, they all come over afterward for breakfast around 10:00. The children bring their favorite gifts to show us, and the conversation is about the great things that happened in their own houses when they awoke on Christmas morning. After breakfast, we gather in the living room with our last cup of coffee or juice and open presents from each other and the friends we've added and, thankfully, great-grandparents and cousins who drop by.

GLORIA GAITHER

chipped beef and gravy

2 (4.5 ounce) jars dried beef
¼ stick butter
1 cup scalding hot water
2 cups milk
2 heaping tablespoons flour
pepper

With kitchen shears, cut beef in narrow strips and place into large skillet • Add butter and water, bring to a boil • Cover and reduce heat to a simmer for 10 minutes to coax the flavor from the meat • Add pepper • Meanwhile, put flour and milk into a shaker and shake until smooth • Gradually add flour mixture to meat mixture over medium heat, stirring constantly • Have extra milk on hand to thin if gravy thickens beyond the consistency of a creamy sauce • Add more pepper if desired (you are not likely to need salt as the dried beef is salty) • Serve in a tureen with a basket of hot homemade biscuits

Gloria with her grandchildren at Christmas time

gaither welcome wassail

Here we come a wassailing!

Nothing smells better when guests walk in out of the December cold than the smell of apple cider and spices perking in the kitchen. And nothing tastes so "welcome" as a sip of steaming wassail from a glass mug with a cinnamon stick floating on the top.

I make this recipe in my big 36-cup silver percolator, and a houseful of company can return again and again for refills all evening. The kids love it, too, after an afternoon of sledding on the hillside or ice skating on the pond.

1 gallon apple cider
1-32 ounce bottle of cranberry juice
½ lemon, scored and cut into pieces
6 to 8 cinnamon sticks
10 to 12 whole cloves
6 to 8 whole allspice
¼ cup rum or 1 teaspoon rum flavoring

In a 36-cup percolator, add the cider and cranberry juice • In the percolator basket place lemon, cinnamon sticks, cloves and allspice • Add rum or rum flavoring and perk as usual • Serve with a cinnamon stick in each cup

GLORIA GAITHER

lela's macaroni and cheese

Bill's mom, Lela Gaither, was the undisputed queen of comfort foods. There was nothing like coming in from the cold to a huge pot of her famous chicken and noodles or her legendary mac and cheese straight from the oven. Others may say they make these dishes, but one taste of Lela's could still the most boisterous of cooks. And as long as we are talking starches, her mashed potatoes could melt the hardest heart and send jolly laughter around any table. Like most great cooks, Lela would give not so much recipes as methods; you know, "a fistful" of this and "a pinch" of that and then knead "until it feels right"— sort of thing.

By the way, all of Lela's granddaughters have this picture framed in their kitchens. They wanted to always remember Lela's hands caressing a batch of noodle dough. This says it all!

GLORIA GAITHER

2 (8 ounce) packages extra sharp cheddar cheese, sliced or cubed
2 cups uncooked macaroni
1 pint half and half cream
butter
cracker crumbs
squeeze bottle liquid margarine or melted butter

Preheat oven to 350 degrees • Cook macaroni until almost tender • Drain and rinse in colander • Butter casserole dish and layer macaroni, then cheese, macaroni, cheese (in layers) until ingredients are used • Pour in half and half cream • Top with cracker crumbs and drizzle liquid margarine or melted butter on top of cracker crumbs • Bake at 350 degrees for 20 to 25 minutes or until top is golden brown

Lela working noodle dough

Lela in her kitchen - where we always found her

andrew's famous chicken piccata

Andrew and I love to cook. We cook for each other, for our children, for our families and for friends. We cook when we are stressed, when we need some time together and when we need nourishment for body and soul. We love good, healthy and satisfying food, preferably from local and organic sources when available. When the weather starts to cool, it's not long before the kids or I request Andrew's Chicken Piccata, which has ruined me for restaurant versions. It's so crispy and lemony, and tender and juicy on the inside, I only want it if Andrew is cooking!

(Modified from The S'conset Café on Nantucket Island)

1 package boneless, skinless chicken breasts
1 cup flour
1 ½ cups bread crumbs, Italian or plain
2 eggs
1 cup lemon juice, fresh squeezed or bottled
½ cup white cooking wine
salt and pepper
5 tablespoons olive oil
5 tablespoons butter

Wash chicken thoroughly • Using a knife, slice across the grain to make thin fillets • Tenderize breasts with a meat mallet • Pat dry with a paper towel • In a large bowl, dredge chicken in flour, egg, then bread crumbs; set aside • In a large skillet, heat 3 tablespoons olive oil, 2 tablespoons butter, ¼ of cooking wine, ¼ of the lemon juice and salt and pepper over medium heat • When butter is melted and liquid starts to lightly bubble, add chicken breasts • Add more olive oil, butter, wine and lemon juice as skillet dries while cooking chicken • Turn each fillet when it is brown or lightly blackened • Remove when crispy and cooked through • Use any remaining liquids to de-glaze the skillet over medium heat and pour over the crisped breasts • Serve with rice, steamed broccoli and Amy's Not-So-Famous Greens and Fruit Salad

Amy and Andrew

Amy Gaither - Hayes, her husband Andrew, and their son, Lee

amy's not-so-famous greens and fruit salad

When we need to bring a dish to a gathering, I almost always bring a salad. You can't always count on there being fresh green veggies at potlucks, and everyone seems to like the fruit, nut and greens mix. I think a salad is not complete without all of those, plus cheese! At the end of the growing season, you can use the last of the lettuces and good grapes are easy to find. This dish goes well with most anything and goes especially well with Andrew's Famous Chicken Piccata.

1 package of romaine lettuce, washed and broken into bite-sized pieces
½ cup of blueberries, raspberries, cut strawberries or grapes cut in half
½ cup feta, gorgonzola or bleu cheese
¼ cup pine nuts
½ ripe avocado, sliced on top
light balsamic vinaigrette

In a large bowl, combine salad ingredients then toss with vinaigrette

Amy with her dad Bill, and her children Simon, Lee, and Madeleine

AMY GAITHER-HAYES

JOY GARDNER

I love collecting recipes and over the past many years have accumulated a cherished assortment. When I first got married, I was not an experienced cook (my mom never wanted us kids in the kitchen making a mess), so I raided her and my sister's recipe boxes. I also began asking my grandmothers, aunts and friends to add to my new collection. At first I cooked everything strictly by recipe, but now I improvise and add a little more of this and a little less of that which makes cooking so much more fun.

As a child I was not a fan of meatloaf – I always wondered what was really in it – but this recipe changed my mind. I have to say, this meatloaf is amazing! Our younger daughter, Lauren, was trying not to eat any red meat, so I tried substituting ground turkey in place of the beef. I thought it was still pretty good, but our older daughter Dionne exclaimed, "What did you do to our meatloaf?" So, needless to say, I went back to good ol' beef. Landy loves to eat around the edges - yes, out of the pan after everyone is finished! I fixed this for Michael English several years ago, and he stills says it is one of his very favorites. I hope you enjoy this recipe as much as we do.

sweet 'n sour meatloaf

meatloaf
1 ½ pounds lean ground beef
1 teaspoon celery flakes
1 heel or slice of bread, dried and crumbled into small pieces
1 medium onion, chopped
1 egg
1 (15 ounce) can tomato sauce
1 teaspoon salt
¼ teaspoon pepper

sweet sour sauce
1 (15 ounce) can tomato sauce
2 tablespoons mustard
1 cup water
2 tablespoons brown sugar, packed
2 tablespoons rice vinegar
1 (15 ounce) can petite diced tomatoes (optional)

Preheat oven to 350 degrees • In a large bowl, combine beef, bread, onion, egg, tomato sauce, salt and pepper; mix well • Shape into a loaf and place into shallow pan or iron skillet • Bake loaf in oven while preparing sauce

For sauce, combine all sauce ingredients in large bowl • Pour ¾ of the mixture over meatloaf, reserving ¼ of mixture for occasional basting • Bake at 350 degrees for 1 ½ -2 hours or until done, basting occasionally

Joy's dining table

vestal's coconut cake

Excerpted from Vestal's personal note to Gloria

This is my most requested and celebrated cake recipe. I've changed it slightly, but believe me, the results are the same. (Ask Bill; the last time he had it, it was from this recipe—basically the same, maybe even better.) When I first made this cake, I had too much frosting, so I said to myself, "This cake needs four layers." So, as soon as the layers cooled, I got me a spool of thread, tore a long strand and started sawing back and forth and made four layers out of two. It was great!

> Vestals Coconut Cake
> I've changed my reciepe
> slightly, but beleave
> me the results are the
> same (ask Bill the last
> time he had mine from
> this one) the same Maybe
> even better.
>   When I first made
> this cake, I had too
> much frosting, so I
> said to myself; This cake
> needs to be four layers.
> so as soon as the
> layers cooled, I got me
> a spool of thread, tore
> of a long string and
> started sawing back &
> forth and made 4
> layers, out of 2. It was
> great,
>   Here tis - - -

Personal instructions as written by Vestal

1 white cake mix, prepared
3 egg whites
1 cup sugar
¼ cup white corn syrup
¼ teaspoon cream of tartar
5 packages frozen grated coconut
milk from 2 fresh coconuts or canned coconut milk
(about ½ cup)

cake
Preheat oven and bake cake as directed on the box in two 9 inch pans • When done, cool, then turn out onto waxed paper, top-side up • cool completely

frosting
Place egg whites, sugar, corn syrup and cream of tartar in the top part of a double boiler and set aside • Bring 2 cups of water to a low boil in the bottom of the boiler • Put the top unit on the double boiler and immediately begin beating ingredients with an electric mixer until it's well mixed • Beat constantly on high for approximately seven minutes as peaks form • Begin icing the first layer of cake and cover with coconut • Continue with each layer • Gently poke 3 or 4 holes into the middle of the cake with a long, sharp knife • Slowly pour in the coconut milk • Cover with a cake cover and refrigerate

Wes Hampton cuts the turkey while Bill Gaither,
Buddy Greene and David Phelps start the feast.

David Phelps and Connie Hopper

Dinner in Greece on the European Tour

The Easter family: (front) Sheri, Maura and Jeff
(back) Madison, Shannon and Morgan

Claude Hopper, Mark Lowry,
Allison Durham Speer, Ben Isaacs and
Ben Speer listen at the *Giving Thanks* taping.

Girlfriends : Sonya Isaacs Yeary,
Gloria Gaither and Ladye Love Smith

The funny Kevin Williams, with
Sheri Easter and Gloria Gaither

Danny, Mary Ann and Vonnie Gaither

Where did this come from? Here are the facts. When we were pastors (from Nov. '57 till Aug. '84), we tried to have potluck dinners at the church pretty often. We would designate who would bring what. On a particular evening, I was to bring a dessert. When I finished my "runnings" and got home, I realized I had at most forty-five minutes to fix a dessert. So I grabbed a chocolate cake mix and prepared it. I said, "Oops, don't have time for layers," so I used a big casserole dish. Now no one expected me to use a jar frosting, so I made up this frosting recipe. When the cake was done I left it in the casserole dish, spread the hot frosting over it, pokin' holes in the cake so the fudge would seep down inside.

I hurried to the church, proudly placed my cake on the dessert table. Brother Jones, a precious older associate, took one look at my cake and said, "Vestal, what kind of cake is that?" I answered, "Don't know yet, haven't named it." He said, "Huh, looks like an ugly cake to me!" So it became my Ugly Cake. And other than the coconut cake, it's my most requested cake. So, eat, enjoy and ignore the calories!

VESTAL GOODMAN

vestal's chocolate ugly cake

1 chocolate cake mix, prepared

vestal's icing
3 cups sugar
¾ cup cocoa
1 (12 ounce) can evaporated milk

Bake a boxed chocolate cake as directed in a glass casserole dish and set aside • Mix sugar and cocoa in a large iron skillet until there are no cocoa balls • Add milk and mix thoroughly • Place on medium heat and stir constantly • As soon as it bubbles lower heat and keep stirring approximately ten minutes • Drop small spoonfuls on a plate to test • When drops stand and are consistency of fudge, remove from heat and add one tablespoon vanilla • Leave cake in pyrex casserole dish • Start pouring hot fudge over the cake, poking holes in the cake so the fudge can seep down inside

Personal instructions as written by Vestal

spoon biscuits

1 ½ cups vegetable oil
2 ½ - 3 cups self-rising flour

Preheat oven to 500 degrees • Grease two iron skillets • In a large bowl add oil and enough flour so that the dough is sticky and doesn't run together when dropped in skillet by large spoonfuls • Bake for 20 minutes or until browned • Turn them out on a plate

Did you ever get up late, and it dawns on you, "We have guests in this house, and they had already said that they had heard I was a good cook?" And you say, "Oh Lord, let me cook breakfast quick!"

I turned on the oven to 500 degrees, hurried and got sausage in the skillet. I grabbed my Tupperware® bowl, poured in a cup and a half of cooking oil, got two iron skillets, greased 'em real good. Then I stirred about two and a half (maybe more) cups of self-rising flour into the oil till it looked thick enough so they wouldn't run together. So I spooned this batter into my skillets one good spoonful at a time (good biscuit size). I hurried up and popped 'em in that hot oven (approximately 20 minutes until they are good and brown), then turned 'em out on a plate. Darlin', from then on it's been the only way I make biscuits. 'Cause they were the bell (biscuits) of the ball (breakfast).

VESTAL GOODMAN

Sam and Stella Goodman, LaBreeska Rogers Hemphill, Vestal with husband Howard, Mama Goodman and Ricky and Vicky (children of Howard and Vestal)

Howard and Vestal Goodman

A few years ago we moved into a house having a basement and a deck – two spaces our old house didn't have. The basement is rightly referred to as the man-cave, where I write, practice, conduct business and do any number of other music related tasks. After three years, it is still a thrown-together eyesore, badly in need of remodeling and redecorating, but I love it nonetheless.

Upstairs the women folk rule, and I'm mostly glad about that. My wife, Vicki, has decorated our home beautifully to feel inviting and comfortable, and it is the place where we are most at ease. When our girls, Erin and Georganna, are home, there's usually some sort of discussion going on between them and Vicki. Occasionally, I might wander upstairs and try to enter into the discussion, but I'm not really good at it. Women are preoccupied with all the wrong things, like clothes for instance, and I naturally make the wrong comment, something like, "Why do you need another pair of jeans?" or "Just because there's a sale going on doesn't mean you have to go shopping." I usually get shouted down and ordered back to the man-cave.

About two or three times a week we like to cook out on that very deck, especially during spring, summer and fall,

but we also grill in winter if the weather allows. It's always an occasion where I'm welcomed into the women's domain, mainly because I am - the grill meister!

Now, I'm old school, preferring the charcoal grill which requires hauling around big bags of charcoal, dousing it with lighter fluid, and starting the fire a half hour ahead of grilling time – all manly tasks that women, for the most part, naturally eschew. But grilling is something I learned from my dad, and something I perform with not a *little* bit of pride, knowing that when executed successfully, will make me, if only for an hour or two, the man of the house – the wise and talented husband/dad, praised and complimented on my extraordinary grilling talent.

We often grill salmon and will have it over a bed of spinach or field greens, or perhaps with grilled vegetables like asparagus or zucchini. I can often talk one of the girls into being my assistant, in order to keep me from running back and forth to the kitchen retrieving utensils, spices or platters I've forgotten to bring in advance.

Of course, the real payoff is the time we spend around the table where I'm actually welcomed into the conversation, or at least tolerated because I've proved myself to be indispensable as grill meister. It's also a great time to realize what an incredibly blessed man I am.

Buddy with his band as a youngster

grilled salmon orientale

3 pounds skinless salmon fillets
3 tablespoons cooking oil
2 tablespoons lemon juice
2 tablespoons soy sauce (or more,
  to taste)
½ teaspoon dry mustard
½ teaspoon ground ginger
⅛ to ¼ teaspoon garlic powder

Place fish in shallow pan • Combine
other ingredients and pour over
salmon fillets • Allow to stand one hour
at room temperature, turning once •
Grease well and preheat grill • Grill
over medium coals to desired
doneness (10 to14 minutes) being
careful to not overcook

ernie's favorite chicken almond casserole

I must confess, I am definitely not a cook. Honestly, I have never really had to cook, so I've just never learned. I do, however, love great cooking! I live in Stow, Ohio, which is also where my wife's family, the Younces, live. To be honest, none of us cook. No one in the entire family, with the exception of my wife's sister, Dana, could cook.

I'm not really sure how she learned, but somehow she did. Momma D, as we affectionately called her, was George Younce's second daughter, and she was a fantastic cook. Unfortunately, she lived in the Atlanta area, and we really didn't get to enjoy her wonderful cooking as much as we would have liked. Needless to say, we loved it when Momma D came home. When George hadn't been feeling well throughout the last few years of his life, Dana would come home quite often. She loved cooking good country meals for her dad. The rest of us just reaped the benefits!

This recipe for Chicken Almond Casserole is one of my favorite dishes that Dana cooked. With all the Younces around one table, you can bet there was a lot of love and laughter as we all enjoyed Dana's good home cooking.

1 cup cooked chicken, chopped
½ cup mayonnaise
1 can cream of chicken soup
1 hard-boiled egg, chopped
1 cup celery, chopped
½ cup toasted slivered almonds
1 teaspoon onion, minced
½ cup potato chips or cracker crumbs, crushed or crumbled

Preheat oven to 350 degrees • Grease 8 x 8 pan or 6 ramekins • In a bowl, combine all ingredients except crumbs for topping • Place casserole mixture in the 8 x 8 inch pan or individual ramekin casserole dishes • Top mixture with potato chips or cracker crumbs and bake at 350 degrees for 20 minutes • Serves 6

Ernie and George Younce at Christmas

ERNIE HAASE

On August 5th, 2009, Ernie Haase & Signature Sound was in Atlanta, GA, doing a TV taping for the Gospel Music Channel, and we had a day off. Instead of working, we spent the day by the pool at my sister-in-law Dana Younce Willis' house. My wife Lisa, and her brother, George Lane Younce and his kids, came over to join us for a big Signature Sound pool party. Dana was in her glory! She absolutely LOVED serving us. That was her gift, and I let her work within her gift. Who was I to stop God from using her by serving me and the boys? HA HA!

This particular day was just perfect – the weather, the food, the fellowship and the peace I had in my heart and mind. I remember thinking to myself that day as I watched Dana do her thing and as I listened to all the guys and kids laughing and splashing in the pool, "This is a perfect day, Ernie...and you are here." What I meant by that was, I was here in my mind and able to recognize the moment and actually be in the moment.

So much of the time, I am thinking down the road – the next big project, the next song, the next business meeting – all the while missing the chance to see God in the moment. I remember saying to myself, "Man, it's good to see the sun," literally and figuratively. I thanked God that we had a great day for this party, and I thanked Him for the rays of warmth on my soul.

The fact is, we know life will have its share of ups and downs, and there are just some days that you cannot feel the warmth of the sun on your life. You feel like you are in the proverbial winter of your life. Little did I know a winter storm was about to blow in the next week.

Just four days after we left Dana, she passed away unexpectedly in her sleep – only 47 years old and gone. I have to tell you, we are still digging out from the after effects of this blizzard that hit our family. Later that year I was able to write about this in a song that hopefully helps people Carpe Diem (Latin for...SIEZE THE DAY!) The song is titled *It's Good to See the Sun.*

Momma D is what I called her. She took care of us all. We are getting by, but life will never be the same. We are sad without her here, but happy she is there – there with her Lord and her daddy George Younce, whom she adored more than words could ever tell. She is basking in the warmth of the eternal light that shines from the Son of God, Jesus Himself.

Momma D's famous Chocolate Sundae Delight is what she served us at the pool party that last day.

Ernie and Dana

momma d's
chocolate sundae delight

crust
¼ cup brown sugar, packed
1 cup self rising flour
1 cup pecans, finely chopped
1 stick margarine, melted

filling
1 cup powdered sugar
1 (8 ounce) package cream cheese
1 ½ cups whipped topping – reserve 1
  cup for topping
1 large package instant chocolate
  pudding
1 small package instant chocolate
  pudding
2 chocolate bars, finely shredded

Preheat oven to 350 degrees • In a large bowl, combine sugar, flour, pecans and margarine in a 9 x 13 inch pan • Bake at 350 degrees for 15 minutes or until golden brown • Allow to cool • Mix powdered sugar and package of cream cheese with a mixer until well blended • Add ½ cup whipped topping to mixture and spread on cooled crust • Prepare pudding mixes according to package directions and spread onto pie • Spread reserved whipped topping on top of pudding layer • Sprinkle shredded chocolate on top for garnish • Chill and serve

rosetta's christmas enchiladas

When Wes Hampton is not out on the road with the Gaither Vocal Band, you'll usually find him in the kitchen whipping up a mean potato soup or chocolate chip Bundt cake. It turns out Wes loves to cook and frequently experiments with recipes, making them his own. When we asked Wes to share a recipe his family traditionally has during the holidays, he sent us...enchiladas? "It didn't start out to be a family tradition, but that is exactly what it has become," explains Wes. "The love of Mexican food and family togetherness makes this recipe a perfect holiday choice for our family, especially on Christmas Eve.

Once the main ingredients are prepared, the whole family gets involved. My wife, Andrea, and her brother Darren grew up helping with this dish, and when Darren's wife, Jennifer, and I both married into the Means family, we were immediately given a spot in the assembly line." It's possible for one person to make the recipe alone, but it is easier if there are two—one to fry and blot the tortillas and one to assemble them. Enjoy!

1 package enchilada sauce mix
1 ½ cups water
1 (8 ounce) can tomato sauce
1 (10 ounce) can enchilada sauce
1 ½ pounds ground beef
1 teaspoon salt
½ teaspoon black pepper
1 (15.5 ounce) can kidney beans
⅓ cup water
1 medium onion, chopped or onion flakes to taste
16 corn tortillas
8 ounces (2 cups) sharp cheddar cheese, grated
canola or vegetable oil for frying tortillas
sour cream (optional)

Preheat oven to 350 degrees • Spray two 9 x 13 inch baking dishes with cooking spray or grease lightly with oil and set aside • In a medium saucepan, stir 1 ½ cups water and tomato sauce and bring to a boil • Add enchilada sauce • Reduce heat and simmer for five minutes or until thickened, stirring occasionally • Coat the bottom of the baking dishes with a thin layer of sauce and set aside until ready to assemble the enchiladas • Brown the ground beef, onion, salt and pepper in a large skillet on medium high heat until completely cooked • Drain • Blend or food process kidney beans and ⅓ cup water • Add blended beans to meat and reduce heat •

Wes cooking

continued

Fry the tortillas one at a time in
¼ inch oil in skillet on medium
high heat for approximately 15-20
seconds on each side • Blot
tortillas dry with paper towel •
Dip in sauce mixture to coat •
Spoon about ¼ cup meat filling
into each tortilla • Roll tortillas
tightly and place in baking dish
(coated with thin layer of prepared
sauce) seam side down, one
inch apart • Top with grated
cheese • Bake enchiladas for 20
minutes or until sauce is bubbly
and cheese is melted • Allow to
stand 5 minutes before serving •
Makes approximately 16 enchiladas

I first had this cake about four years ago at a family reunion in Texas. I remember Andrea and me eating about half of the cake ourselves, so I just had to get the recipe! Andrea's grandmother's niece had made it, and she graciously gave us the recipe. I've made a couple of changes to it, but it is basically the same. This cake has become a favorite of our family and friends, and we hope you enjoy it. It was also one of Anthony Burger's favorites, so I think of him every time I make it.

chocolate chip bundt cake

1 package yellow cake mix
1 (3.9 ounce) package instant chocolate pudding
2 tablespoons cocoa powder
½ cup sugar
8 ounces sour cream
¾ cup vegetable oil
¾ cup water
4 eggs
1 ½ cups mini semi-sweet chocolate chips

Preheat oven to 350 degrees • Grease fluted bundt pan • Combine first four ingredients in a large bowl and mix until well blended • In a separate bowl, whisk together sour cream, oil, water and eggs until thoroughly blended • Turn on mixer and gradually add the wet mixture to dry mixture, stopping halfway through to scrape sides of bowl, being careful not to over mix • Once mixture is combined, fold in chocolate chips • Pour mixture into prepared fluted bundt pan • Bake for 50-55 minutes • Allow cake to rest for 20 minutes

Wes's son Barrett, helping out in the kitchen

My wife Andrea LOVES cheesecake, and when I started cooking years ago, it was mainly entrées. But the baking bug bit me, and I started experimenting with cakes. I made a chocolate chip bundt cake, carrot cake and coconut cake. The day I made my first cheesecake was a good day in the Hampton house. I added Oreo® cookies to the cheesecake and that made it an even better day! It was Andrea's birthday cake one year and my mom's birthday cake another year. The boys have a sweet tooth like their father and can knock out this cake even quicker than Andrea can!

oreo® cheesecake

oreo® crust
1 stick unsalted butter, melted
1 package oreo® cookies
1 teaspoon salt
1 tablespoon sugar

oreo® filling
2 pounds cream cheese, room temperature
1 cup sugar
1 teaspoon salt
4 large eggs
1 cup sour cream
8-10 oreo® cookies (or more, if you prefer),
  coarsely crushed

Preheat oven to 375 degrees • Butter a 9 inch springform pan along the bottom and sides • In a food processor or gallon bag, pulse or crush cookies with salt and sugar until combined • Slowly pour in the melted butter until combined • Press crust mixture into bottom of pan, going up the sides to one inch • Using the bottom of a glass, press mixture down firmly • Bake for 13 minutes and allow to cool • Reduce oven temperature to 325 degrees • Fill a 9 x 13 pan half-full with boiling water and set on bottom rack in oven • With a mixer, beat cream cheese on medium speed until smooth, scraping down sides of bowl • Add sugar and beat until well-combined •

The Hampton family

WES HAMPTON

continued

Add eggs, one at a time, and mix after each until combined • Fold in cookies to cheesecake mixture • Pour filling into the pan and bake on middle oven rack for 1 hour and 40 minutes to 2 hours, center will be set when done • Remove from oven and allow to cool for 30 minutes • Run a paring knife along the sides to release cheesecake from the sides of pan • Allow to cool and refrigerate overnight • Garnish with remaining oreo® cookies

mitzy's chili

Our family loves getting together around the holidays. As we start telling stories around the fireplace, nothing hits the spot during those cold Kentucky winters like a steaming hot bowl of chili with all of the fixings. Unfortunately, the body doesn't take a break on holidays so I still try to fix healthy, heart-friendly meals. When you're spinning yarns and enjoying family, no one wants to think about dieting... or even eating something that tastes like you are dieting. So here's a solution to try. Larnelle and our bunch love it.

P.S. Don't tell our son Lonnie, daughter Teresa, or our grandkids that this recipe calls for turkey instead of beef. In fact, "mums the word" for your family, too. It will be our little secret!

Mitzy Harris

1 pound ground chuck
1 pound ground turkey
1 package chili seasoning mix, hot
1 package chili seasoning mix, original
2 (15 ounce) cans chili with beans
1 (28 ounce) can crushed tomatoes
2 large white onions, chopped
7 cups water
3 servings whole wheat spaghetti
1 teaspoon salt (for cooking pasta)
salt, pepper and chili powder to taste

Bring six cups of water to a boil in five quart pan • Add one teaspoon of salt and drop in spaghetti • Reduce heat slightly as not to boil over • Brown turkey and beef in large skillet • Add salt, pepper and chili powder to meat as it browns • While cooking, stir and break meat into small pieces • When almost fully browned, add chopped onion and seasoning packages along with one cup of water • Mix well and allow to simmer on low heat • After spaghetti has been cooked to desired consistency, drain and add back to pot along with both cans of chili • Stir and mix well • Add crushed tomatoes and meat mixture and simmer for about 10 minutes, stirring occasionally • Serves 6 to 8

Larnelle and Mitzy

LARNELLE HARRIS

The simplest meals, prepared by loving hands, give a family a sense of well-being when shared together. Having been raised in the home of grandparents, I had the privilege of knowing a time when the kitchen table held the most important position in the house. Waking up to the smell of Mama Goodman's homemade biscuits browning in the oven, fat back bacon sizzling in the big iron skillet, and the aroma of coffee perking in a much used and very worn coffee pot was a daily happening at our house. In those days there was no such thing as skipping breakfast; you couldn't help being lured into the kitchen by the mouth-watering aromas and the hum of activity. Mama Goodman's homemade pear preserves made this more than just breakfast; it was an event, and not one bite was taken without first "asking the blessing" over what God had so graciously provided.

At the house of Mama Rogers, my paternal grandmother, it was the supper table I remember most. We could always count on cornbread, coleslaw, butter beans and iced tea with lemon. No matter what else was served we could count on these being on Mama Rogers' table at supper time.

When our children were at home, I kept the deep freeze full of fresh vegetables from the farmers' market, canned bread and butter pickles and homemade fig preserves. When we were in Pennsylvania in concert, I would have the driver stop the bus and buy tart cooking apples to freeze for making "apple crunch." And when we were in Georgia, we stocked up on peaches for winter treats.

Now that the children are all married and away from home, it is important to me that they all come to the house often for a meal. Sometimes I fix lunch and call Joey and Trent over when they take a break from their bus business, or Candy and Kent and the children when they are back in town. But supper is my favorite time because it is not so rushed. Every few weeks we have a bigger family gathering at our house which includes extended family and friends, and I often serve duck gumbo.

How rewarding it is to share a meal with those we love and have all six grandchildren around us. How could I put a price tag on such an occasion? I know it will take a lot of work and time to plan and pull off a big meal like this, but the dividends far exceed the investment I make in time and energy.

What the grandchildren really like is when Uncle Trent, or Uncle Howard or our niece Dixie goes to the piano and we all burst out in song. When the weather calls for it, we have a roaring fire in the fireplace, but what really warms our hearts is the wonderful sense of belonging when we all gather in a big circle and talk of God's mercy and faithfulness in our own personal walk with Him.

LaBreeksa Rogers Hemphill at age 7

duck gumbo

3 ducks
1 fryer chicken
1 package smoked sausage, chopped
1 bunch green onions, diced
1 bell pepper, chopped
3 stalks celery, chopped
salt and pepper to taste
cayenne pepper to taste
filé (powdered seasoning), to taste
1 package creole gumbo mix
½ package frozen okra, chopped
½ cup flour
rice, cooked

In a very large pot or kettle boil ducks and fryer until done • Remove skin and bones from ducks and fryer • Add meat back into the stock* • In an iron skillet, brown sausage and drain; add to stock • Sauté onion, bell pepper and celery in some sausage drippings; add to stock • Pour remaining sausage drippings in skillet and brown flour; add to stock • Add salt and pepper to taste • Add okra and bring to a boil • Add about ⅓ bottle filé just before serving and stir very little after that • Serve over hot rice • Serves 12

*This can even be done the day before and stored in refrigerator. You can also substitute all fryers for ducks.

There is nothing more important to me than having family and friends at the house for a relaxed evening of food and fellowship. Joel and I are like most everyone else; we live such a fast-paced life we hardly have time for anything, and if we aren't careful, relationships get lost in the shuffle. It takes real effort to make time for each other, but it's well worth the effort.

When we have a supper at the house it usually includes friends who are in town for one thing or another: ministers, gospel singers, promoters, etc. For instance, the Sullivans, who play bluegrass gospel, are longtime friends who live in Alabama. Every time they come this way, Brother Jerry will call beforehand to say they'll be in town. If we are in town at the same time, we have a big gathering at the house. I have a few special dishes I prepare and usually order several chickens or brisket from the barbeque place. Then Joel starts calling friends in town. Gordon Jensen, Henry and Hazel Slaughter, LaVerne and Edith Tripp, and Ray and Laura Lewis are some of our regulars.

Joel and I absolutely love having our friends over; and whoever comes, we always wind up at the piano. It's really something when the bluegrass pickers come with all their instruments. It's also great to get to hear new songs our friends have just written.

These valuable times cannot be measured in dollars and cents; but they do cost in time, effort and a few dollars. I know when I set aside a night to entertain it usually takes a whole day out of my busy schedule, but I do it gladly for the sake of friendships. Joel and I travel to encourage and bring hope to a wounded world through song and testimony. It would be a shame to neglect our family and friends.

But the biggest investment we'll ever make is in our children and grandchildren, and we are still making deposits. I am more aware than ever of how short a time I have to pour my values, my faith and my philosophy for living into my grandchildren. The best way to do that is to have them around me.

This is a favorite dessert I have been serving both friends and family for years. Joel calls it LaBreeska's Delight. It is delicious, and the surprise is the toasted nut crust. I always tell new guests, "Be sure and dig down to the crust." When they take a bite, you can see it hit them. I like that.

LABREEKSA HEMPHILL

LaBreeska and her grandchildren

labreeska's delight

1 ¾ cups flour
1 ¾ sticks butter, melled
1 cup nuts, chopped
1 (8 ounce) package cream cheese
1 ¼ cups powdered sugar
1 (8 ounce) container whipped topping
1 (3 ounce) package vanilla instant
  pudding mix
1 (3 ounce) package chocolate instant
  pudding mix
cold milk for pudding, follow package
  directions

Preheat oven to 350 degrees • In a large bowl, mix flour, butter and nuts • Pat into bottom of a 9 x 13 baking dish • Bake at 350 degrees for 25 minutes or until brown • Let cool and set aside • Combine cream cheese, powdered sugar and half of whipped topping in a bowl • Spread on cooled crust • Make chocolate pudding as directed on package • Pour over cream cheese mixture and repeat with vanilla pudding • Top with the remaining whipped topping • Chill and serve

joe's special

Whenever Daddy was in San Jose, CA, he made a stop at Original Joe's.® He would always order Joe's Special. Mama was with him on one of his trips, and Daddy made her order the Joe's Special as well. They sat at the counter and watched as their meal was prepared. The cook told them the recipe, and the Hess family has eaten it ever since. Though the exact recipe was never recorded, it goes something like this.

Becky Hess Buck,
Jake's daughter

1 pound ground chuck
1 box frozen spinach
2 medium onions, chopped
1 clove garlic
2 eggs
olive oil
salt and pepper to taste

Drain spinach and squeeze out as much water as possible, set aside • Add olive oil to coat bottom of skillet • Brown onions and garlic • Add meat and sauté until meat loses all redness • Slowly stir in spinach • Break two eggs into skillet and stir constantly until eggs are set • Serve immediately

JAKE HESS

Jake with his wife, Joyce, and daughter, Becky

For me a recipe has to taste fabulous but must be simple and easy to prepare. Texas Spicy Rice Casserole is just that, and it keeps showing up on the Hildreth table year after year. My daughter, Kathryn, cooks it when we gather at her home for a special meal. Watching her bring this tasty dish from the oven to the dining table brings back a rush of sweet family memories.

When Kathryn and her brother, David, were just starting to school, my schedule with the Singing Wills Family was really demanding. My wonderful husband, Howard, made sure our children had a normal lifestyle. His job as a movie theatre manager enabled him to get the kids to and from school and care for them until I could get home from singing with the Wills Family. I learned to prepare meals that could be warmed in the oven, long before the microwave was invented. I was given the recipe for this rice casserole on one of our singing trips to San Antonio. It is easy to make and will keep in the refrigerator. Kathryn tells me now that it was served often at that modest little home in Fort Worth, Texas.

In the early sixties, Kathryn, David and Howard joined the Singing Wills Family troupe, and the next few years were some of our happiest times. Our television series "Wills Family Inspirational Time" was shown in major markets, and we traveled on our bus to many cities for Friday and Saturday concert dates. Sundays found us on the church platform of some pastor friends on our way back to Texas. On Mondays, Tuesdays, and Wednesdays, the Hildreths sat down to home-cooked meals. The meals were simple, but we were glad to be home and thankful for God's blessing on our gospel singing family. Today our hearts overflow with gratitude when we are together for a special meal, and we can count on Kathryn to cook Texas Spicy Rice Casserole.

Lou Hildreth with her daughter, Kathryn Hildreth Mumaw

LOU WILLS HILDRETH

texas spicy rice casserole

3 cups long grain white rice, cooked
freshly ground pepper and dash of
  salt, to taste
3 cups sour cream
1 teaspoon salt
1 (7 ounce) can diced green chilies
12 ounce block monterey jack cheese,
  sliced or grated
½ cup cheddar cheese, grated

Preheat oven to 350 degrees • Grease
1 ½ quart casserole dish • Season
cooked rice with salt and pepper; set
aside • In a large bowl, combine sour
cream, salt and chilies • In the
prepared casserole dish, place a layer
of rice, followed by a layer of the sour
cream mixture • Top with strips of
Monterey Jack cheese • Repeat,
making 2 or 3 layers, end with rice on
top • Bake at 350 degrees for 40-45
minutes, or until thoroughly heated •
Sprinkle cheddar cheese on top of
casserole and return to oven until
cheese is melted • Serves 4 to 6

In Texas, Mom Wills' barbeque is legendary. The customers who stopped at Calvin's Barbeque came for the generous heaping of beef, topped with the tastiest sauce to be found. Besides a satisfied appetite, folks hung around for the kindness of our gentle mother. My older brother, Calvin, had opened the little shop on Main Street in Arlington, Texas, to help the Wills Family with money to travel and sing the gospel. Mom cooked the sauce early every morning in a big pan, and Calvin loaded the meat to be cooked. We had the Wills Family Music Store next door, and all the younger brothers and sisters worked either at the barbeque place or in the music store during the summer and after school. This allowed us to travel on weekends and tour in the summer. Pop Wills helped Mom a lot, but when the Wills' bus left town he was on board. He was the founder of the Singing Wills Family, and he was proud of his kids.

Down the street from the barbeque were the fire hall and the police station. The firemen and policemen were daily customers and loved Mom's cooking. Even when she knew she was dying with cancer, she came to the little shop to make the barbeque sauce and check on her regular customers. At her funeral, the firemen asked to be honorary pallbearers, and the Arlington Police Department led the funeral procession with a squad of motorcycle officers. Mom's barbeque sauce was served with so much love and compassion. She not only influenced her sons and daughters, but she left her mark on a Texas town. Calvin sold the barbeque shop years ago, but people still talk about eating with Mom. Pop Wills is gone too, but both of our parents gave us the passion for serving people and singing gospel music.

LOU WILLS HILDRETH

Pop and Mom Wills

The original Singing Wills Family: Lou, Bob, Calvin, Norma Joe, and Betty

mom wills' barbeque sauce

½ cup catsup
½ cup vinegar
2 tablespoons chili sauce
3 tablespoons mustard
2 tablespoons worcestershire sauce
1 cup water
1 tablespoon salt
½ teaspoon pepper
3 tablespoons brown sugar
1 teaspoon liquid smoke
1 cup melted butter or cooking oil

In a sauce pan, mix together all ingredients • Heat to a low boil to blend flavors • Use or cool and store in refrigerator (keeps for two weeks) • Yields 3 cups

connie's easy delicious coconut cake

Quite a few years ago our group was invited to the home of a gracious couple for Sunday dinner. The hostess served this delicious coconut cake for dessert. We kept raving about how wonderful the cake tasted. She said, "It's quick and easy and will keep in the fridge for days." She gave me the recipe and I often make it for our family gatherings. It's as quick and easy as that dear woman said. I also enjoy giving this cake as a gift to friends.

1 package yellow cake mix, prepared
1 (14 ounce) can sweetened condensed milk
1 (15 ounce) can cream of coconut
1 large bag coconut flakes or fresh coconut

Preheat oven to 350 degrees • Grease 9 x 13 baking dish • Prepare and bake yellow cake mix according to package directions • While cake is baking, mix condensed milk and cream of coconut in a large bowl until smooth • After cake has been removed from oven, immediately poke holes in entire cake using a fork • Slowly spoon the coconut mixture on the cake making sure the mixture seeps into holes • Spread coconut on top of cake • Let cool and refrigerate • The cake will keep for several days in a refrigerator

CONNIE HOPPER

Thanksgiving is usually a family day, celebrated with big dinners, joyous reunions, and special church services of worship, praise and prayer. The very mention of Thanksgiving often calls up memories of kitchens and pantries crowded with good things to eat.

My first Thanksgiving dinner as a young bride and a new cook is not very memorable. Claude's job had moved us to Kentucky temporarily. Normally on Thanksgiving Day, the Hopper brothers – all eight – and their dad would go hunting in the morning, returning in the afternoon to enjoy a delicious feast that Mom Hopper had prepared. This particular year, it was just Claude and me far from home in a small apartment, and I attempted to prepare my first Thanksgiving dinner.

I had watched my mom many times as she prepared baked chicken or turkey and the most wonderful dressing in the world, so I thought I'd try and do it just like she did. Usually, the chicken came from a pen in our back yard, but eventually my dad found it easier to go to the local grocery store, and we graduated to a nice plump turkey. I knew that Claude and I would need only a small chicken, though I had never seen a small one being prepared. I fully intended to boil my three pound chicken just as many hours as Mama boiled her 15 pound hen turkey, but after a couple of hours the meat was perfect for chicken casserole. I had never heard of chicken casserole 48 years ago.

The local supermarket in Hopkinsville, Kentucky, sold pole beans instead of green beans. I had never eaten any, so I thought I'd give them a try, but I could hardly stand the odor as they were cooking. Needless to say, nobody gobbled them up. I don't remember what I did to the yams, but I do remember the expression on Claude's face as he came in from work (not from the customary hunt), and we sat down to that wreck of a Thanksgiving dinner.

Claude was kind as he smiled and nibbled at his food; I smiled and nibbled too. Today we can laugh about it, and thank goodness, the cooking has improved some. Over our 49 years of marriage, I have prepared numerous 13-20 pound turkeys with dressing for our children, grandchildren and huge extended family. I'm not sure it has ever been as good as my mama's. Honestly, in a pinch, I have resorted to grocery store brands of dressing, but nothing beats "from scratch." Whatever the circumstances, Thanksgiving is special and about gratitude – a matter of heart.

CONNIE HOPPER

Connie and Claude on their wedding day

Claude and Connie Hopper

southern cornbread dressing

cornbread
1 egg
¾ cup milk
1 tablespoon vegetable oil
1 cup self rising corn meal

dressing
cornbread, crumbled
6 slices bread, toasted
1 cup celery, diced
1 medium onion, finely chopped
4 tablespoons butter
4 cups broth
salt, pepper, sage and poultry
   seasoning to taste

For the cornbread, preheat oven to 450 degrees • Grease iron skillet or bread pan • In a large bowl, blend all ingredients well • Pour batter into prepared pan • Bake at 450 degrees for 12-17 minutes • Remove from oven and cool

For the dressing, preheat oven to 325 degrees • Grease 9 x 13 baking dish • Crumble cornbread and toast in large mixing bowl • In a skillet, sauté onion and celery in butter until tender • Add sautéed onions and celery to bread mixture along with 4 cups broth (stew chicken for broth or use packaged chicken broth) • Mixture should be very moist • If too dry, add more broth • Add salt, pepper, sage and other seasonings if desired • Pour mixture into prepared baking dish • Bake at 325 degrees for 45-50 minutes or until top is lightly browned

A southern tradition is to place a skillet on stovetop and cover bottom with oil • Drop spoonfuls of dressing mixture into hot skillet and fry until golden brown

Chocolate has always been considered a "comfort food;" it can mend broken hearts, fill a void, and place a smile on your face.

My grandmother, Snow Townsend, was one of the sweetest and most significant ladies in my life, not just the example she set as a committed, Godly woman, but she is the reason I sing. I remember countless hours of practicing harmony parts at the church and in Granny's hair salon. Needless to say, being able to talk about her is a complete honor.

Granny died from pneumonia in 1936 when mom was only eight years old. With the twelve kids her father was now raising alone, his meager food stamps salary didn't leave much for treats and extras. Around the age of ten, mom and her sisters, Clara and Stella, were determined to create something sweet and tasty on what little means they had. They spent days in the kitchen concocting and mixing to finally come up with what we now know as "chocolate gravy."

The mixture is almost the taste of chocolate pie filling with the consistency of gravy. For my granny and her family, it was an easy fix for a sweet tooth, but by the time she began making it for my mother and her siblings, it had become a staple for the Townsend family breakfast. Now, for me and my family it's a treat and a tradition on holidays, especially when Granny is there.

Kim Hopper with Granny Snow and Carolyn Greene (Kim's mom)

DEAN HOPPER

granny's chocolate gravy

3 tablespoons flour
½ cup sugar
pinch of salt
2 tablespoons cocoa
2 cups milk

Mix dry ingredients in medium sauce pan until well blended • Whisk in milk and cook on medium heat until it begins to boil, stirring constantly • Simmer 10 minutes or to desired consistency • Serve over piping hot biscuits

drop in soup

The other day a fellow was telling me about the old house where he grew up. He said it was in terrible shape. I said, "I'll bet I lived in a house one time that was worse than yours. The roof on our house leaked so bad that when it rained, it took two hours to eat a bowl of soup."

Now when this soup recipe is ready, I always make a big batch of cornbread. Then I call my children, who live close by, and say, "We got soup, why don't you 'drop in' and have a bowl."

1 pound lean ground turkey or lean ground beef
½ head green cabbage, chopped
1 large sweet onion, diced
1 (8 ounce) can creamed style corn
1 (8 ounce) can lima beans
1 (8 ounce) can tomatoes, italian style with juice
1 or 2 cans of water (for thicker soup, use less water)
3-4 medium potatoes

In a 5 quart soup pot, sauté the cabbage and onion in olive oil • Just before browning, add the turkey or beef • Cook until meat is browned, stirring often • Add canned vegetables and potatoes • Cover and simmer until potatoes are fully cooked • Add salt and pepper to taste • Allow the soup to settle and flavors to blend before serving

Carl as a Hazel Green High School Bullfrog sophomore - hair today... gone tomorrow!

CARL HURLEY

baked oatmeal

The first time I ever had baked oatmeal was when the Isaacs were singing in Pennsylvania. We were staying at Jonas and Anne Beiler's bed and breakfast. (Anne is the Anne of Auntie Anne's® Pretzels so you know whatever she served was going to be fantastic!) We woke up to this delicious dish. I love sharing new recipes with my wife and children, so I asked Anne for this one. She graciously shared it, and my family just loves it. It's a new favorite of ours, and I'm sure it will become a favorite for you and your family too!

1 ½ cups quick-cooking oats
½ cup sugar
½ cup milk
¼ cup butter, melted
1 egg
1 teaspoon baking powder
¾ teaspoon salt
1 teaspoon vanilla extract

Preheat oven to 350 degrees • Grease 9 x 13 baking dish • In a large bowl, combine all ingredients; mix well • Spread mixture evenly in prepared dish • Bake at 350 degrees for 25-30 minutes or until edges are golden brown • Immediately spoon into bowls • Top with any of your favorite oatmeal toppings: warm or chilled milk, brown sugar, fresh fruit, canned fruit, nuts, raisins

BEN ISAACS

Cameron, Mindy, Kyra, Jacob and Ben

hymie's lasagna

I only have one brother. His given name is "CHIAM," which means..."life" in Yiddish. He went by the name HY but our family always, affectionately, called him "Hymie." He is five years younger than me, but we have always been very close.

Shortly after I got married and left New York City, I moved to Ohio to start a new chapter in my life. My brother, who was away at Alfred University in New York State, came to visit me for a week. I never realized he was such a good chef! One evening, he surprised us by fixing dinner. What he cooked was the most amazing lasagna I had ever eaten. After much prodding he shared his recipe with me.

He currently lives in Novato, California, with his wife Sue and two children, Alice and Nathan. Although miles do separate us, I always miss him. I never fail to think of him when preparing this dish!

To this day it is one of our family favorites. In fact, it has become our Christmas dinner tradition. We always have lasagna for Christmas. To this feast, I always add crusty garlic bread, a huge tossed salad and maybe a hot apple pie!

LILY ISAACS

1 (13.25 ounce) box lasagna noodles
1 (48 ounce) jar traditional spaghetti sauce
1 (14 ounce) can tomato sauce
2 (16 ounce) bags mozzarella cheese, shredded
1 (8 ounce) bag mild cheddar cheese, shredded
1 (8 ounce) jar of shredded parmesan cheese
2 pounds lean ground beef
garlic powder, salt and pepper to taste

In a large pot, cook lasagna noodles on medium heat until tender • Strain noodles and set aside • In a large skillet, brown ground beef with generous amounts of garlic powder, salt and pepper until meat is done • Add enough spaghetti sauce to cover meat and simmer for 15 minutes on low heat • Preheat oven to 375 degrees • In a 9 x 13 glass pan, add tomato sauce to cover bottom of dish • Add one layer of lasagna noodles over sauce • Add layer of meat mixture • Add layer of spaghetti sauce • Add a layer of each of the three cheeses using mostly mozzarella, a little cheddar and a little parmesan • Repeat process until all ingredients are used • Sprinkle remaining parmesan cheese on final layer • Bake at 375 degrees for approximately 20-30 minutes • Be careful not to over brown cheese

Lily and Hymie

noodle kugel

One of my favorite recipes was handed down to me from my grandmother, Faye Fishman. It is a Jewish dish that she learned to make from her mother in Poland. I remember as a child we would go to visit my grandmother, and I couldn't wait until dinner was served because I knew she would make my favorite Noodle Kugel for dessert. Even to this day when Grandma knows I am coming for a visit, she makes this dish for me.

REBECCA ISAACS BOWMAN

1 (12 ounce) bag thin egg noodles
4 eggs
1 stick butter, melted
1 cup sugar
pinch of salt
1-2 apples, chopped
1 (15 ounce) box white or golden raisins
cinnamon to taste

Cook egg noodles as directed on the package, drain and set aside • Preheat oven to 350 degrees • In a large mixing bowl, mix eggs, butter, sugar and salt; mix well • Add apples and raisins to the mixture • Fold in cooked noodles • Spread butter in a 9 x 13 baking dish • Add Noodle Kugel mixture to the dish • Sprinkle with more cinnamon on top to taste • Bake at 350 degrees for 45 minutes or until top is nicely browned

Grandmother Faye
with Ben, Becky
and Sonya

Connie Hopper, Joy Gardner and
Russ Taff enjoy a joke.

Bill and Gloria Gaither in Ketchikan, Alaska

Glen Payne with David and Chonda Pierce

Ben Isaacs, Gene McDonald, Gordon Mote
and Bill Gaither telling a great story
at the Alaskan Salmon Bake

Around the Thanksgiving table at
The Fontanel Mansion in Nashville, TN.

Jeff Easter lookin' forward to lunch

Danny Gaither at a "Race Day" picnic
at the Gaither homestead

Charlotte and Greg Ritchie with kids, Landon and
baby Jayna, on a Homecoming Alaskan Cruise

grandma faye's rugulach

If you're wondering what in the world rugulach is, you obviously haven't paid a visit to many traditional Jewish bakeries! Rugulach is a delicious rolled cookie-like pastry with just the right amount of cinnamon and sweetness, a perfect pastry for dipping in coffee. This particular recipe comes from my Grandma Faye.

I love to remember the family trips made each December from Ohio to our grandparents' home in the Bronx. Grandma would spend days shopping, cooking and preparing for our arrival. She knew what hearty appetites we had! And after spending as much "quality car time" as we could stand, we would rush into Grandma's apartment, get smothered in plentiful hugs and kisses and head straight for the kitchen table!

When we didn't think we could possibly eat another bite, Grandma would go to her secret stash and pull out a few plates of rugulach. Suddenly, no one remembered the long uncomfortable hours of riding in the car. We were at Grandma and Grandpa's, and it was a time to eat and be merry!

To this day, rugulach takes me back to those young years when life was carefree and you could eat whatever you wanted—without guilt!

SONYA ISAACS YEARY

4 cups self-rising flour
2 (8 ounce) packages cream cheese, softened
2 sticks butter
¼ cup walnuts, chopped
⅔ cup red raspberry or strawberry jam
1 tablespoon cinnamon
2 tablespoons sugar
¼ cup raisins or chocolate chips

In large bowl, mix together flour, cream cheese and butter • Knead dough and separate mixture into four round balls • Refrigerate overnight • Remove dough from refrigerator and flatten balls out with floured rolling pin into thin pizza like circles • Preheat oven to 375 degrees • Add thin layer of raspberry jam, then sprinkle dough with walnuts and raisins (or chocolate chips) • In a small bowl, mix cinnamon and sugar • Sprinkle cinnamon sugar mixture onto flattened pastry • Slice into approximately 3-4 inch triangles and roll each triangle from the wide base to the point (similar to a croissant) • Sprinkle tops of pastry with cinnamon sugar mixture • Bake at 375 degrees for approximately 20-25 minutes or until golden brown

Sonya (front), and Becky (in the doorway) with cousins, Heidi and Holley, making mud pies in the playhouse

God is smart. He makes little boys love tough things like trucks, sports and hunting. And to balance life, He gives little girls an innate preference for dress-up, dancing and cooking. Ever since I can remember, I have loved the idea of cooking, especially baking! I used to love to visit at my cousin Holley's house in Ohio where she, her little sister Heidi, Becky and I would spend hours out back in their playhouse kitchen. We put everything we could think of – dirt, grass, water, weeds – into our "delicious homemade pies." It didn't matter how much our concoctions looked like mud, in our minds they were all "'sugar, spice and everything nice!" Fortunately, I did spend a little time in Mom's kitchen and learned the real ingredients for the best apple pie I've ever eaten. The secret, as you will find, is in the sugar cookie piecrust topping. Enjoy!

lily's crumb topping apple pie

ingredients
frozen deep dish pie shell
5 small to medium apples
½ cup sugar
1 teaspoon cinnamon
5 pats butter, 1 ½ teaspoons each

sugar cookie dough topping
1 or 2 (9 ounce) boxes pie crust mix
⅓ cup sugar or splenda®
½ stick butter

Peel and thinly slice apples • Put apples into bowl, along with sugar and cinnamon and lightly toss • Pour apple mixture into frozen pie shell • Dab 5 pats of butter evenly on top of pie • Add a pinch of flour if the apples are really juicy to absorb some of the juice

Preheat oven to 385 degrees • In a large bowl, melt ½ stick of butter • Add ⅓ cup sugar to butter and mix while hot • Pour in a box of pie crust mix • Stir and knead until mixture is doughy • Using your hands, crumble the dough mixture on top of the pie topping • Bake at 385 degrees for 50-60 minutes • Bake on a cookie sheet to catch juices that may bubble over • You may need to cover the pie with foil halfway through baking to keep the crust from burning • You can double the topping if you prefer

JEANNE JOHNSON

My grandmother was a very strong woman. She worked all her life in a cotton mill, which was very physical work. I can remember seeing her with her clothes wringing wet after walking home from the mill. She raised six children, including my father, and went off to work everyday to do a very strenuous job. Even with all this, she was willing to take in two other young children to raise as her own. My parents divorced when I was five, and it was decided my brother, Larry, and I would be better off at Grandma's house. She was a strict woman and took us to church every time the doors were open. That's when I learned that Jesus loved me in spite of any feelings of rejection or disappointments, and He had a plan for my life. Somehow Grandma got the money for me to take piano lessons, and I took the lessons for about eight years. My love for music grew through those years, and at some point along the way I realized I could sing a little, too. Later God put a great man in my life, Bob, who is a former marine. We married and had a beautiful daughter, Sonja. She married and had two daughters of her own, Kylie Faith and Kaylie Hope. They are the bright lights in my life. When I was growing up those many years ago, I would watch Grandma come home after a long day at work and whip up the best meals ever! I just wish she had written down all those recipes. This cherry cobbler is one that stands out in my mind. I hope you enjoy it. It's wonderful served warm with vanilla ice cream. As best as my Aunt Joan and I can remember, this is how she made it.

Grandma and Grandpa Poteat with little Jeanne and her brother, Larry

Bob and Jeanne Johnson

grandma's cherry cobbler

1 cup self-rising flour
⅔ cup shortening
3 ½ tablespoons cold water
¾ cup sugar
2 tablespoons butter
1 (14.5 ounce) pitted tart red cherries,
   (canned in water - do not drain)

Preheat oven to 400 degrees • In a large bowl, combine flour and shortening • Mix with fork or pastry cutter until crumbly • Add water a little at a time until a dough is formed • Dust pastry board and rolling pin with flour • Roll out dough from center in light short strokes to abut ¼ inch thickness • Pour cherries and liquid into an iron skillet or oven-safe pan • Sprinkle sugar over cherries • Cut dough into thin strips and lay across cherries in one direction • Press dough strips down into cherries and juice • Lay additional dough strips in opposite direction over first strips • Press into cherries and juice • Lay any remaining strips of dough crisscross over other strips again pressing into cherries and juice • Cut butter and put on top of cobbler • Cook on top of stove on medium heat and bring to a boil for 3-4 minutes • Remove from burner and place in oven • Bake at 400 degrees for 20 minutes or until top is browned • Remove from oven and again press top of cobbler into cherries and juice

After my parents divorced, my Aunt Opal and Aunt Joan, along with my grandparents, played a huge roll in my growing up years. Many times Aunt Opal gave financial help when things were needed for Larry and me. Both of these women were dependable and trustworthy people.

I remember when the time came for students to get their class rings, Grandma couldn't afford it, but Aunt Opal gave me the money. Aunt Joan was there for me many times, too, for personal things I needed. God always provided through these women.

Several years ago Aunt Opal became very ill and was in and out of hospitals. Many days I drove from our home in Charlotte to Raleigh to be with her, picking up Aunt Joan on the way. Aunt Joan and I cooked and cleaned for her and would sit many hours reminiscing about things that had happened in our family through the years. I loved those times. In one of those conversations, Aunt Opal told me about a recipe for peanut butter pie. In fact, she had one in the freezer, and we ate it that day. It was scrumptious! When I got home, I tried it out on Bob. He loved it, too!

I thank God for the people in my life when I was a child. Had it not been for their love and guidance, my life could have taken a totally different direction. God always knows what's best for His children.

JEANNE JOHNSON

Aunt Opal

peanut butter pie

2 prepared graham cracker crusts
1 cup peanut butter
½ cup skim milk
1 cup confectioners sugar
1 (8 ounce) cream cheese
1 (12 ounce) container whipped topping

In a large bowl, combine peanut butter,
milk, sugar and cream cheese • Mix
well • Fold in whipped topping • Pour
mixture into graham cracker crusts
and freeze • Move to refrigerator one
hour before serving

I am definitely the exception to the "southern-woman-cooking-comes-naturally" thing! Born and bred in Nashville, a descendant of several great southern women cooks, I am still only a wanna-be. I have stacks of *Bon Appétit* and *Gourmet* magazines that I keep alongside my collections of cookbooks – not that it changes the fact that I'm pretty much a culinary illiterate. But truly, just the cooking experience in general is an absolute treat for me. I light candles and line up bowls in my kitchen. I buy the weirdest array of mushrooms and herbs and all the stuff you aren't supposed to eat (real sour cream and butter and all those fattening, fabulous ingredients), and I dive into the recipes like I know what I'm doing. Some of the time, I even fool my kids, the pets and my ever-patient husband. "You're going to love this!!" – and the fact that everyone is starving – works most of the time.

When I was in high school, the mom of one of my best friends was a gourmet cook. Leslie's mom is one of the most fascinating women I've ever known. Leslie's father was the president of Capitol Records and helped the Oak Ridge Boys and several other talented artists (such as Barbara Mandrell) find a

place to record and be "discovered." But the greatest thing about Leslie's parents was that they opened their home to me and my other strange, art-driven teenage friends during a time in our lives when we needed nurturing emotionally, physically and spiritually. At Leslie's house seven or eight of us would do plays and sing and write bad songs. We so needed someone to listen, and her supportive parents would applaud and encourage us. One of the best memories I have is of the gorgeous and elegant tables Leslie's mom would set with china and crystal and lighted candles. Here we were, a bunch of smelly teenagers, being treated like we were real people who mattered on this earth.

Leslie's mom, Toni, made many, many amazing meals for me over the years. My favorite is Linguini with Clam Sauce, the recipe for which I begged and finally got in her own hand writing – a treasure to me. From the first dinner party I ever hosted (sweating all the way) until now, I have loved making and serving this dish because it is a slam-dunk winner every time!

Here is the recipe. May you love it and enjoy it as I have.

Bonnie (on right) with her best friend, Leslie.

BONNIE KEEN

linguine with clam sauce

½ cup olive oil
2 cloves garlic, thinly sliced
2 (7.5 ounce) cans clams
1 tablespoon freshly chopped parsley
   or parsley flakes
1 teaspoon salt
½ teaspoon oregano
½ teaspoon pepper
1 (16 ounce) box linguine, cooked

In a large pot, cook linguine according to package directions; drain and set aside • In a skillet, slowly heat olive oil • Lightly brown the garlic cloves in oil • Slowly stir in ¾ cup of the juice from the cans of clams (make sure to add a little at a time and be sure your oil is not too hot) • Discard remaining clam juice • Slowly stir in parsley, salt, oregano and pepper • On a cutting board, mince the clams and slowly add them to the mixture • Bring to a gentle boil, cover and remove from heat • Serve over freshly cooked linguine • Serves 4 to 6

my mother's japanese fruit cake

This is an old recipe handed down through the family for generations. When I was a child, this cake was a Christmas tradition, and that is the only time of the year we had it. My sister and I always helped mother make it as there were no pre-shelled walnuts or frozen coconut in the grocery stores. We had to shell the walnuts, help grate the coconut and take turns stirring the batter. It was a tradition we looked forward to every year, but the best part was eating it. When it was gone, we would scrape the plate.

This recipe is different from other fruit cakes. It is very moist and delicious to the last bite. To borrow a phrase from *The Christmas Carol*, "It was a triumph."

cake
1 cup butter, melted
2 cups sugar
4 cups flour
1 cup milk
4 eggs
1 teaspoon baking powder
1 teaspoon vanilla
1 teaspoon cinnamon
1 cup seedless raisins
1 cup citron
1 cup walnuts

icing
1 small can crushed pineapple
juice of one small orange
rind of 1 orange, grated
1 package frozen coconut
3 cups sugar
1 cup boiling water
2 tablespoons cornstarch
3 tablespoons butter
pinch of salt

cake
Preheat oven to 300 degrees • Grease and flour four cake pans • In a bowl, add melted butter, sugar, eggs, milk, flour and baking powder; mix well • Add vanilla, nuts, citron and raisins • Bake in greased and floured pans • Makes four layers • Bake for 35-40 minutes at 300 degrees • Allow cake to cool completely before icing

icing
Combine all ingredients except cornstarch in a large saucepan over medium heat • Dissolve cornstarch in ½ cup cold water • When mixture begins to boil, add cornstarch • Continue to cook, stirring with wooden spoon constantly until mixture

Ginger as a little girl with her sister and parents

∽ continued ∾

thickens to spreading consistency •
Allow to cool, then spread icing
between layers and on remainder
of cake

My dear mom, Helga Leithaug (pronounced light-houg), came across the Atlantic to visit the USA as a young housewife back in the 1950's. I first moved to the USA in 1989. This recipe for a Norwegian apple cake, or "eplekake" as we say, came with me in my limited luggage. I made sure my handwritten cookbook from 8th grade home economics at Meland Ungdomsskule, by Bergen, Norway, made the trip with me.

I have now lived in the USA for many, many years, so my family is very familiar with the emotions of living far from each other geographically. Once when my mom was seated next to a high-level politician at an official dinner, she asked if he could please pass a new law to make it illegal for grandchildren to live on another continent! Though the visits are limited, I treasure the heritage Mom and Dad have given me; love for God, family, music, literature, nature, and a deep appreciation for the body of Christ, and yes, food.

When hosting dinners in our home, my husband, Jim Chaffee, is truly the chef in the family, while making the desserts falls to me. The apple cake is one of our favorites, and my son, John, even requested I make it for his 9th birthday. I typically place the cake in the oven a few minutes before dinner is served. After 35 minutes or so, the apple cake is done. Serve it warm, paired with a scoop of vanilla ice cream, and you have a wonderful treat. Did I mention the aroma? It smells heavenly, and it reminds me of Mom.

SOLVEIG LEITHAUG

**Solveig (on right)
with her Norwegian family**

mom helga's
norwegian apple cake

3 eggs
11 tablespoons softened butter
  (1 tablespoon short of one and a
  half sticks)
1 ⅓ cups sugar
1 teaspoon baking soda
1 ¾ cups unbleached flour
3-4 apples, cut in wedges
2 tablespoons cinnamon
2 tablespoons raw or refined sugar

Preheat oven to 350 degrees • Grease
11 x 17 or 9 inch round cake pan with
butter • In a large bowl, combine
butter, eggs and sugar • Using an
electric mixer, beat mixture on high
speed for two minutes • Add baking
soda and flour to butter mixture and
mix on low speed for an additional two
minutes • Gently pour batter into cake
pan • On a plate mix cinnamon and
sugar • Dip the apple wedges coating
both sides • Gently place apples on
cake batter • Bake at 350 degrees for
30-40 minutes or until crust is golden

In the early days of the Statesmen, my dad was pastor of a small country church, Mt. Zion Baptist, located near Atlanta. My parents were often invited to eat with members of the church after Sunday morning services. Mrs. Frank Brooks, wife of one of Dad's deacons, would prepare this dish for Dad and Mom when they were invited to the Brooks' home. This recipe was one of Dad's favorites and is still used often at our family dinners.

Lisa Lister Walton, Hovie's daughter

scalloped asparagus

2 (10.5 ounce) cans green asparagus tips
1 stick butter
4 tablespoons all-purpose flour
pinch of salt and pepper
4 hard boiled eggs, sliced
¾ to 1 cup milk
½ cup cracker crumbs, heaping
1 tablespoon melted butter

Preheat oven to 325 degrees • Melt butter in large saucepan • Stir in flour, salt and pepper • Add milk gradually to desired consistency and cook, stirring sauce continually until mixture is thick and smooth • In casserole dish, place a layer of asparagus, then eggs, then sauce • Add another layer of each: asparagus, eggs and sauce • Make buttered bread crumbs by crushing crackers to equal a heaping half cup and stirring in one tablespoon melted butter • Top casserole with buttered cracker crumbs and bake at 325 degrees for 8-10 minutes or until crackers lightly brown

(From left to right)
Doy Ott, Denver Crumpler,
Hovie Lister, Wade Creager
(orchestra leader), Jake Hess,
Executive from Nabisco®
(Statesmen's T.V. sponsor)

HOVIE LISTER

beverly's microwave pralines

My mother always makes these at Christmastime, but I think this is the perfect thing to make the next time you have a dark night of the soul. You never know when one of those "dark nights of the soul" is gonna hit. They come on pretty fast and can last for days, so it's best to have these ingredients in your cupboard at all times. I make them for myself often, and they are really good.

Yep, there's nothing like Mama's Microwave Pralines on a "dark night of the soul" kinda day. Or, just because it's Tuesday.

1 (16 ounce) box light brown sugar
2 tablespoons light corn syrup
1 cup whipping cream
1 tablespoon butter
2 cups chopped pecans

In a large microwave safe mixing bowl, combine brown sugar, corn syrup and whipping cream • Using microwave, cook sugar mixture on high setting for 13 minutes • Remove from microwave and add butter and chopped pecans • Beat candy mixture until creamy • Using a teaspoon, drop mixture onto waxed paper or pour into 8 x 8 buttered pan and cut into squares when cool

The Lowry family

MARK LOWRY

beverly's divinity

Bill always says about this Homecoming bunch, that we are part-time singers and full-time eaters. If you were raised in the same church I was, you would know that eating is about *all* you were allowed to do. But you were allowed to do a lot of it. It was growing up at The Berean Baptist Church in Houston, TX, where I first learned that great food plus great friends equal great conversation. Fifty-two years later I still believe it. There is something mystical that happens when you eat with friends; you let your guard down, you open up, and you can time your most shocking statements for just that moment when they're about to swallow - and you zing 'em. It's fun to watch 'em choke. Butmake sure you know the Heimlich maneuver before you attempt this!

I never tried that little trick with George or J.D. or Vestal. They were a little old for the choking, but the conversations were always entertaining. Hovie and Bill loved to reminisce about the good ol' days when The Statesmen were king...Bill still does. We all loved to eat, and with the eating came the fellowshipping, and it's in the fellowshipping that life is lived to it's fullest.

Here is a great recipe from the Lowry home. Enjoy!

2 ½ cups sugar
½ cup white corn syrup
½ cup cold tap water
pinch of salt
two egg whites
1 teaspoon vanilla
½ cup nuts

In a saucepan over medium heat, stir together the sugar, corn syrup, cold water and salt stirring only until sugar has dissolved • Cook sugar mixture until it reaches a temperature of 250 degrees on a candy thermometer • While syrup is cooking, beat the egg whites until stiff peaks form in a large bowl

Once the sugar mixture has reached a temperature of 250 degrees, carefully pour a slow stream of candied sugar into beaten egg whites, beating constantly at high speed • Add vanilla and continue to beat until mixture holds its shape, approximately 4-5 minutes • Fold in nuts • Using 2 spoons, drop the mixture onto wax or parchment paper, using 1 spoon to push the candy off the other spoon • Cool completely • Store in airtight container

MARK LOWRY

grandma's green jell-o® salad

1 large package lime jell-o®
1 small can crushed pineapple
1 cup small curd cottage cheese
1 tablespoon mayonnaise, whipped into cottage cheese
½ cup pecan pieces

Pour juice of pineapple into measuring cup and add water to equal 2 cups • In a medium bowl dissolve lime gelatin with one cup hot water • Add pineapple water mixture, crushed pineapple and cottage cheese; blend and stir • Sprinkle with pecans and refrigerate until set

MARK LOWRY

grandma's sugar cookies

When I was a kid, we did things together as a family. When we would go over to Grandma's house, we would eat and then play music until late at night. Pop played the piano, and Grandpa would play the fiddle. Friends would come over with guitars, and we would sing all night, and Grandma would give me some spoons so I could keep the rhythm. Mom would sing, and my sister, Pop and I would join in. We would sing old hymns quite often, and I can remember those nights like they were yesterday. You see, my family was the most important thing to me. My parents and grandparents were my heroes, and I had a sister who taught me a lot about singing...and love. It was Grandma's cooking that brought us all together. We would sit, eat, laugh and talk about anything and everything that was happening in our lives. Grandma's sugar cookies were always available just because she knew I loved them. Grandma seemed to always have food ready within 5 minutes of the family's arrival, whether or not she knew we were coming. This has always been a fond family memory for me.

Gospel music is also my "family thing." If we all stick together like family, we can deal with most anything. Next time you see me giving someone a hug, remember that it's a "family thing."

1 egg
1 stick margarine
1 cup sugar
½ cup pecans or nuts, chopped
1 cup self-rising flour
1 teaspoon vanilla

Preheat oven to 325 degrees • Grease cookie sheet • Mix all ingredients in a large bowl • Flour both sides of the cookie dough • Roll out dough with a rolling pin to about ¼ of an inch thick • Use a drinking glass to cut out the cookies and place onto floured parchment paper • Bake for 12 minutes at 325 degrees

GENE McDONALD

Gene with his parents, Tommy and Doris, and his sister, Janeene

beef tenderloin and marinade

In 1994, Carol and I were looking for a special treat at Christmas for our family Christmas dinner. Our first grandchild had been born on December 21, 1994, and we wanted to celebrate his birth with a special family meal. The decision was made to have another main meat dish (along with the turkey and ham). Carol wanted to do a beef tenderloin, and she created this marinade for the meat. Since then, this has become the FAVORITE main dish at every family holiday meal. Now there are more kids at the table on Christmas.

5-6 pounds beef tenderloin
1 cup soy sauce
⅔ cup vegetable oil
3 tablespoons brown sugar
2 tablespoons dijon mustard
1 tablespoon white vinegar
1 teaspoon garlic powder
1 green onion, chopped
¼ cup red cooking wine
4 tablespoons worcestershire sauce

In a large bowl, combine all marinade ingredients and stir • Make sure the tenderloin has been trimmed of extra fat • Put tenderloin and marinade in a large resealable bag • Refrigerate for at least 8 hours, turning bag often • When ready to cook, preheat oven to 400 degrees • Remove tenderloin from bag and place on wire rack in a large pan • Insert a meat thermometer into the thickest portion of the tenderloin • Bake tenderloin at 400 degrees until it reaches the desired temperature on the thermometer (175-180 degrees) for medium to medium well • Use marinade to baste the tenderloin as it cooks

GARY MCSPADDEN

McSpadden family Christmas

momma moscheo's macaroni pie

My Italian mother was an excellent cook. Her food was very simple but delicious, and prepared with the best ingredient, her love! My dad would make out the menu for the coming week each Sunday night. I can see him now as he listed his favorite dishes, and we kids couldn't wait once we saw the menu. All the dishes were so good and very Italian!

As a side dish, not even the main course, Mom would make one of her specialties and we named it "Macaroni Pie." It was our favorite because you could eat it later, or take a slice to school the next day; that is, if there was any left over!

Mealtime was so special at our house, and because my loving parents were such beautiful Christian people, they made sure my brother, my sister and I knew how fortunate we were to be raised in a Christian home and to have our mom as our 'cook.' Home is such a fond memory for me, and I cherish those times in my life! Thanks Mom and Dad Moscheo. (Mom if you're watching, send down some M-Pie; I miss YOURS. Somehow, when I make it, it tastes different!

(the Italians called all sized noodles...'moc-a-'roni')

6 eggs, beaten
2 cups fresh ricotta cheese
1 pound pasta of your choice

Cook the spaghetti as directed • When cooked, remove from heat and drain well • Do NOT rinse • In a large mixing bowl beat eggs • Fold in ricotta cheese until well blended • Pour over the "noodles" (American for spaghetti) and gently stir • Into a large greased skillet, pour in spaghetti mixture • Cook until first side is golden brown on low to medium heat • Put a plate over the half cooked "pie," and flip it over so that you can slide the uncooked side back into the skillet • When that side is brown, slide it onto a serving dish • Cut it like a pizza, in wedges

JOE MOSCHEO

Joe with his mom

the best turkey ever

Some of my very favorite childhood memories are of gathering each year at my aunt's house on Christmas Day. We always enjoyed playing with cousins and grandparents and of course, partaking in the great feast that seemed to take all day to prepare! Oh, I could hardly wait to taste the turkey and dressing with cranberry sauce and the sweet potato casserole with the yummy marshmallows on top. Then there was the corn pudding and Mom's famous green bean casserole. Perhaps the highlight of the meal was my granny's Mississippi Mud Cake. Mmm, I can almost taste it now!

Funny though, I also remember the conversations in the car on the way home about how everything was so delicious... except for that darn dry turkey. I guess I never really understood the big deal about the turkey. After all, wasn't turkey supposed to be dry? Well, as an adult who loves to cook and eat, I made it my mission to find the secret to a perfectly moist and delicious roasted turkey. Heaven forbid that people have conversations on their way home about my dry turkey! So, after researching and testing different recipes, I found the one. I know this, because every year Gordon says, "Honey, this is the best turkey I have ever tasted." And I believe him.   *Kimberly*

2 cups morton's® kosher salt
2 cups sugar
2-3 gallons of cool water
1 (12-15 pound) fresh, whole, bone-in, skin-on turkey, rinsed and patted dry
8 tablespoons unsalted butter, divided (5 tablespoons softened; 3 tablespoons melted)
½ teaspoon ground black pepper
1 cup white wine or chicken broth

brine
Combine kosher salt and sugar in cool water in a large stockpot until completely dissolved • Place whole turkey in brine until completely submerged • Cover and refrigerate four to eight hours minimum, or up to 24 hours for best results • Remove turkey from the brine, rinse inside and out under cool water for several minutes to remove all traces of salt • Pat dry with paper towel

roast
Preheat oven to 450 degrees • Mix the softened butter with pepper • Place turkey on rack in roasting pan • Rub the seasoned butter under the skin • Brush the skin with the melted butter • Pour one cup liquid (wine or broth) over the pan bottom to prevent drippings from burning • Roast turkey at 450 degrees for 25 minutes • Baste, then rotate

Gordon's wife, Kimberly

~ *continued* ~

pan • Continue roasting until the skin turns golden brown • Roast for an additional 25 minutes and baste again • Reduce oven temperature to 325 degrees • Continue to roast turkey, basting and rotating the pan once about halfway through cooking until the internal temperature of the turkey reaches 170 degrees for breast meat and 180 degrees for thigh meat • Remove turkey from the oven • Allow to stand 20 minutes before carving

BUDDY MULLINS

Shirley Davis, affectionately called Aunt Shirsha, was a precious woman of God known in our church for all the meals she prepared for widows, widowers, the poor and just anybody that needed them. That was her gift back to God; to love on and cook for people, and she was an awesome good ol' homestyle southern cook.

Both my grandparents on my dad's side passed away when I was very young, and Shirley and Coy adopted our family for many occasions, but specifically Thanksgiving dinner. We became so close to them through those times that I asked them to stand in at our wedding as grandparents on my dad's side. They both were very special to Buddy and me. Shirley made the best cornbread dressing in the church, and when she passed away suddenly of an aneurysm in 2007, several women, including her daughter Pam and my mother, came together and made Shirley's special dressing for lunch on Sunday. It became a friendship luncheon where about five couples plus her husband, Coy, (affectionately known as "Coke man") gathered together to share a meal once a month. Aunt Shirsha's special dressing is still on the menu every Thanksgiving.

Kerri Mullins

aunt shirsha's cornbread dressing

6 cups homemade cornbread, crumbled
6 biscuits or 6 slices white bread, crumbled
1 medium onion, chopped
3 large celery stalks, chopped
6 hard-boiled eggs, chopped
1 (10.75 ounce) can cream of chicken soup
2-3 (14.5 ounce) cans chicken broth
Salt, pepper, and sage to taste

Preheat oven to 375 degrees • Grease 9 x 13 baking pan • In a skillet, melt butter and lightly sauté onion and celery • Mix all ingredients except broth in large bowl • Slowly add broth until mixture is the consistency of wet sand • Bake uncovered at 375 degrees for approximately 45-60 minutes or until lightly browned

Buddy and Kerri Mullins with Aunt Shirsha

JIM MURRAY

cherry oatmeal dreams

I was raised in Michigan, and even though I have lived for over 40 years in Tennessee, I still look forward each winter season to all of the traditional holiday things we once did and still do as a family. One of those special things is making my favorite cookies. My mother, Jan Murray, passed on a recipe that we at the Murray home still prepare just in time to break our New Year's resolution to cut back on sweets.

Lorretta and I are passing this tradition on to our three granddaughters, who I pray by the time they can cook will prepare these cookies for us in our old age!

I asked my mom when she had first made these cookies. She answered, "1949," to which I replied, "Was I born then?" I must have been because I have remembered these delightful winter treats over the years. I hope all who make them will enjoy them also.

3 cups of all-purpose flour
½ teaspoon salt
1 teaspoon baking soda
2 cups quick oats plus additional for rolling
1 cup butter
1 ½ cups sugar
2 eggs, beaten
1 tablespoon maraschino cherry liquid
1 teaspoon vanilla
½ cup maraschino cherries, cut into quarters
1 cup walnuts, chopped

Preheat oven to 350 degrees • Grease cookie sheet • In a large mixing bowl sift flour, salt and baking soda • Add oats and set aside • In a separate bowl, cream butter and sugar • Add eggs, cherry liquid and vanilla to butter mixture; mix well • Add the dry ingredients (minus the oats) to wet mixture; mix well • In another bowl add quick oats for rolling • Shape flour and butter mixture into balls using a melon ball scoop • Roll each ball in the oats until coated • Insert a piece of cherry in the center of each cookie • Bake at 350 degrees for 15-18 minutes

Lorretta and Jim

kentucky pie

1 deep dish pie crust, unbaked
1 cup sugar
½ cup flour
2 eggs, beaten
1 stick melted butter
1 cup pecans or walnuts, chopped
1 (6 ounce) bag semi-sweet chocolate chips

Preheat oven to 325 degrees • In a bowl, combine all ingredients; mix well • Pour mixture into unbaked pie crust • Bake for 60 minutes

Having been raised in the great state of Michigan for the first 18 years of my life, the average, everyday kind of food I ate back then consisted of things like meat loaf, mashed potatoes and gravy and some type of salad, with a piece of bread or a dinner roll. In 1963 I met my future wife, Lorretta, and my eating habits changed forever. She was born in Michigan, but all of her summers were spent in Kentucky.

I remember the first time I ate with her at a family gathering; they put on some kind of feast! Two or three kinds of meat and vegetables I had never heard of were common fare. I've eaten things that were pickled, smoked, breaded and seasoned with meat grease, and I have survived. The best part of the family gathering was always the dessert table. You'll notice I said "table" because there was never just one dessert to choose from. One of my favorite desserts is the following recipe that Lorretta would make for me as a treat. It always reminds me of when we were first dating over 46 years ago, and I would go to her home after church for a meal. I hope you enjoy this easy to make "Kentucky Pie." Bon appetite!

JIM MURRAY

Jim and Lorretta

granny's icebox cookies

This is my grandmother's recipe. She is 88 years old, and she never really uses exact measurements for her ingredients, but we did the best we could to make her "little dab of this, a pinch of that, and a spoonful of this" into a real recipe. When I was a little girl, the first thing I did when I got to her house was to get one of her icebox cookies.

I always loved going to her house up in the mountains of North Carolina. Her life has always been like her recipes; a little of this and a bit of that in random measure. She was never too busy to sit down and play with us, and like her recipes, she would throw in a little laughter, a listening ear, a tender hug, and enough love to go around for everyone. She is a shining example of the best recipe for a Christian life.

I hope you enjoy these cookies as I have down through the years. May they remind you as they have me to take time for loving, laughing a lot, and enjoying immensely what each day brings.

Proverbs 31: 30-31 "Charm is deceptive, and beauty is fleeting; but a woman who fears the Lord is to be praised. Give her the reward she has earned and let her works bring praise at the city gate."

KELLY NELON

1 cup melted butter
2 cups sugar
2 eggs, slightly beaten
3 ½ cups flour

Preheat oven to 375 degrees • Grease cookie sheet • In a large bowl, cream butter and sugar together • Stir in slightly beaten eggs until well blended • Slowly mix flour into butter mixture • Shape into two inch diameter logs • wrap in plastic wrap and refrigerate for 1 hour • Slice into ¼ - ½ inch slices and bake at 375 degrees for 8-10 minutes

You may keep this dough for a few days in the refrigerator or freeze it up to 6 weeks. Be sure to double-wrap dough in plastic wrap. When you are ready to bake, let the dough defrost in the refrigerator

Granny with Kelly Nelon

pineapple pudding

sugar-free

2 sleeves plain graham crackers, crushed
2 (16 ounce) cans crushed pineapple, drained
2 small boxes sugar-free cook and serve vanilla
  pudding, prepared
1 large box sugar-free instant vanilla pudding, prepared
sugar-free whipped topping

Layer one sleeve of crushed graham crackers in a 9 x 13 pan • Pour one can of crushed pineapple over the crackers • Prepare the cook and serve pudding according to package directions and pour over the pineapple • Add a second layer of crushed graham crackers and the second can of drained pineapple • Prepare the instant pudding according to package directions and spread over pineapple layer • Top with the sugar-free whipped topping

coconut pie

sugar-free

1 prepared graham cracker crust
2 small boxes instant sugar-free vanilla
  pudding
3 cups milk
½ to 1 teaspoon coconut extract
2 packages frozen coconut
sugar-free whipped topping

Prepare pudding according to package directions, adding in coconut extract • Fold in coconut • Spread onto graham cracker crust • Allow to cool • Top with sugar free whipped topping

Joyce and Calvin on their wedding day

CALVIN NEWTON

black walnut apple cake

This black walnut apple cake is just about the best dessert I've ever had. Unfortunately, I've developed diabetes in recent years – probably because I have eaten too many desserts at church dinners! Joyce has created some really delicious sugar-free desserts that continue to satisfy my sweet tooth! This black walnut apple cake is *not* sugar - free, but is so delicious that I sometimes indulge in a small piece and make up for it elsewhere!

CALVIN NEWTON

cake
2 cups sugar
1 cup vegetable oil
3 large eggs
1 teaspoon salt
1 teaspoon baking soda
3 cups all-purpose flour
2 teaspoons vanilla extract
3 cups granny smith apples, peeled and diced
2 ½ cups chopped black walnuts

brown sugar glaze
1 cup brown sugar, packed
½ cup butter
⅔ cup evaporated milk

Preheat oven to 325 degrees • Grease desired cake pan(s) • In a large bowl, combine sugar, oil, eggs and salt • Beat at medium speed until well blended • Add baking soda and beat 2 minutes • Gradually add flour and beat until combined • Stir in vanilla, apples, and one cup walnuts • Bake at 325 degrees for 45-50 minutes (for two layers) or 50-60 minutes (for 9 x 13 or bundt) • Cool for 10 minutes then remove from pan • Let cool one hour as you prepare the glaze

For the glaze, combine sugar and butter in small saucepan over medium heat stirring until butter is melted and sugar is dissolved • Stir in evaporated milk and bring to boil, stirring for 2-3 minutes or until thickened • Remove from heat and chill for one hour • Spread brown sugar glaze over cake • Press remaining black walnuts into top and sides of cake

Calvin at a church dinner

Calvin and his daughter, Jackie

Gene McDonald and Madison Easter with Sonya
Isaacs Yeary stealing a bite from Greg Ritchie

Homecoming group with Bill Gaither,
Mark Lowry, Kim and Dean Hopper

Giving thanks

Janet Paschal and Jake Hess at lunch on tour

Gloria Gaither visits with Bill's sister, Mary Ann, as kids make Thanksgiving afternoon crafts.

Gordon Mote makes a menu suggestion to Kevin Williams.

Gary McSpadden with Lela and George Gaither at a Homecoming taping at Gaither Studios

Bill Gaither with Ladye Love Smith, Reggie and their son, Bret, at the Alaskan Salmon Bake

The Oldhams have many favorite family recipes...as you can imagine. However, the list topper would have to be our version of the Russian dish "Stroganoff." It is a wonderful feast of flavor in a tomato base instead of a white gravy base.

When my sister Karen was getting married, the day arrived when our family was to meet the "in-laws" to be. My mother, in her typical way, created a glorious dining room with great thought going into every detail. Best 100 year old "Lincoln" china, beautiful hand stitched linens, pewter mugs with matching porringers for fruit – well, you get the idea. The meal chosen for these special guests from New Jersey was our favorite, Stroganoff. Since it can be served over rice or noodles, she had prepared both, along with individual loaves of homemade bread. Our company arrived, and while we put on the finishing touches, my dad, ever Mr. Hospitality, showed the family around our home and then took them outside to see the grounds and pool area. When the candles were lit, Momma, with us in tow, went out to say, "Dinner is served." As we all made our way into the house, the aroma of this culinary event filled every nook and cranny.

Allowing the guests to enter the dining room first, we heard a gasp in unison, and we all appeared wide-eyed to see the issue at hand. There was Charlie Brown, our Irish Setter, on top of our hand carved table for 14! His head was completely submerged in the large antique tureen filled with Stroganoff, one foot in the butter and the other foot in the bowl full of rice! We were so stunned we all stood there in silence watching this sweet, clumsy pet enjoying the heck out of our meal! Finally, Harry, the father of Karen's fiancé, said, "Steak anyone?" As I recall, he paid for our dinner that night at a local restaurant. These two families have shared many memorable times together since that fateful evening. Some of these times have caused us to stand in stunned silence while others have caused us to erupt in roof-raising laughter! Such is the way with families.

Rebekah Oldham Cox

Charlie Brown

DOUG OLDHAM

beef stroganoff

3 pounds round steak cut ¼ inch
 thick strips
4 tablespoons flour
salt and pepper
1 large onion, chopped
1 teaspoon dry mustard
1 teaspoon worcestershire sauce
1 (29 ounce) can tomato sauce
1 (4 ounce) can mushrooms
1 package frozen peas
1 cup sour cream

Cut steak into strips • In a re-sealable bag add flour, salt and pepper • Put steak strips into bag and shake to coat both sides with flour mixture • In a large skillet brown strips on each side • Place browned steak and onions in a dutch oven • Sprinkle with mustard and worcestershire sauce • Add tomato sauce, cover and simmer on stove top or in oven for 2 hours • Remove from heat, add peas and mushrooms and allow to cool for 10-15 minutes • Gently fold in sour cream • Do not add sour cream while stroganoff is too hot as it will curdle • Serve over noodles, rice or toast

baked sloppy joe sandwiches

There's a rumor that I have been dubbed "Buffet Queen of Gospel Music." I'm not sure that's true, but Doug and I surely have hosted many such occasions and enjoyed doing so. Success always begins with the basics—a simple but profoundly practical rule of thumb. Begin by taking a walk around your table and deciding where to lay out your cutlery and plates. Choose a recipe that is simple and not too messy, and don't forget the napkins. I sometimes do a sloppy joe sandwich with the usual chips, pickles and olives. I'm sharing this baked sloppy joe sandwich recipe that should be served warm, and it is not messy.

Gloria and I (before we knew better) once served a soup buffet. She made two soups and I made two. We gathered lots of bowls, spoons and crackers, then invited more people than we could seat. We were ready! I must say it was a smashing success; so much for dumb luck! By the way, you don't have to spend money on flowers for decoration. Pick some weeds and spray them silver and gold; put them in an old crock or wooden box and you are all set. Old books make a good display, or you might use song books, highlighting one or two of your favorite songs. It makes a good conversation starter. Most importantly, enjoy your own party and everybody else will too!

3 pounds hamburger
1 pound sausage
2 cups dry breadcrumbs, crumbled fine
2 or 3 onions, finely chopped
2 tablespoons worcestershire sauce
3 teaspoons salt
1 quart tomato juice

Preheat oven to 350 degrees • In a large bowl combine all ingredients; mix well • Pat mixture into shallow baking pan • Bake at 350 degrees for 1 ½ - 2 hours, stirring often • Bake until thick and not too sloppy • Remove from oven • Makes about 20 sandwiches

DOUG OLDHAM

Doug and Laura Oldham

grandma carroll's tea cakes

One summer day when Ivan was a young boy, he waited on the ice cream truck to come by his house; however, he missed it. When a neighbor saw him and his cute expression, she had to take a picture. Ivan went inside his home and told his mom that he had missed the truck, and he began to cry. Their family of nine, with Ivan being the youngest of seven kids, did not have a lot but they made great use of everything they did have. There was a tremendous amount of love in this family, so his mom decided to make his favorite cookies which she called "Tea Cakes." They were inexpensive to make and were always a very special treat for Ivan.

Teresa Parker

4 eggs
3 cups sugar
1 cup milk
1 pint melted lard or shortening
4 teaspoons baking powder
2 teaspoons vanilla
4 to 5 cups flour

Preheat oven to 350 degrees • Grease cookie sheet • In a large bowl, combine shortening and sugar; mix well • Add eggs individually to sugar mixture and beat after each addition • Add vanilla • In a large bowl, mix flour and baking powder • Gently add flour mixture to wet mixture adding just enough flour for manageable dough • Drop cookie dough by spoonfuls onto prepared cookie sheet • Bake at 350 degrees for 20-30 minutes or until golden brown

IVAN PARKER

Ivan missing the ice cream truck

pigs in a blanket

When we were first married, Squire was a school teacher and was paid only once a month. Needless to say, as a young wife, shopping and making things for supper for a month at a time was challenging.

As the month stretched on, Squire would get up in the morning and scan the fridge and cupboards for what could be "supper." The last morning of one month, he found the following ingredients and off to school he went – knowing we wouldn't starve. Not to be daunted, my "Susie homemaker" thing kicked in, and I lovingly made "pigs in a blanket." I even thought of dessert – biscuits and apple butter – and proudly waited to serve him and be praised for my ingenuity.

Linda Parsons

1 small can biscuits (6)
1 cheese slice
2 hot dogs
apple butter (optional)

Slit hot dogs length wise and cut each in half, making four pieces • Put ¼ cheese slice inside of each cut piece • Wrap each in a biscuit • Bake as directed, including the two extra biscuits • Serve warm

SQUIRE PARSONS

Linda and Squire Parsons

key biscayne lime pie

This Key Lime Pie recipe is the uncontested, all-time favorite of my husband, John. And he should know key lime pie; John grew up in Florida, where his dad pastored churches on the mainland and in the Keys. He has taste-tested dozens—no, make that hundreds—of pieces of key lime pie and has pronounced mine the best! The test of the best in the key lime variety is the color; great flavor is found in those pies that are whitish-yellow. If it's green, it's a dead giveaway the recipe has been corrupted by the addition of green food coloring or gelatin!

This pie is creamy and tart and can be decorated with a few sprinkles of graham cracker crumbs or grated lime peel. Enjoy!

4 eggs, separated (reserve 3 egg whites for meringue)
1 (14 ounce) can sweetened condensed milk
½ cup key lime juice
2-3 teaspoons grated lime peel
1 baked 9 inch pastry shell
½ teaspoon cream of tartar
½ cup sugar

Preheat oven to 350 degrees • In a large bowl, beat egg yolks; stir in milk, lime juice and grated lime peel • Beat one egg white until stiff • Fold into pie filling mixture • Gently pour into pastry shell • Beat reserved egg whites with cream of tartar until foamy • Gradually add sugar, beating until stiff but not dry • Spread meringue on top of pie, sealing carefully to edge of pie shell • Bake at 350 degrees for 15 minutes or until meringue is golden brown • Cool until room temperature • Chill before serving

JANET PASCHAL

Janet Paschal backstage

london broil by nancy

My sister and I grew up next door to our cousins. We were each born in October, one year apart. Kay and Nancy were in the same grade, as were Wanda and I. We attended our grandfather's church, exchanged gifts at Christmas, and went trick-or-treating in town—a giggly foursome that enjoyed ringing the doorbells. As the years passed and we went our separate ways, we saw each other only at Christmas.

John and I had just moved back to North Carolina when I became sick in 2005. One day the phone rang, and Wanda said that she and Nancy wanted to come for a visit. Kay joined us, and on the first day we talked about six hours. We had a lot of years to catch up on, and we enjoyed every detail. When I started feeling better, we ventured to restaurants, malls and vacation spots.

Five years later, we still meet regularly for dinner. In that time, we have laughed until we could hardly breathe, borne each other's burdens and bared our own souls. What a treasure we have found. What a gift they are. Nancy shared her recipe for London Broil with us, and I prepare it on a regular basis. Enjoy - then call an old friend and set a date for dinner.

2 – 2 ½ pound london broil or other beef roast
meat tenderizer
1 envelope onion soup mix
1 can cream of mushroom soup
water

Preheat oven to 350 degrees • Place meat in large baking dish • Sprinkle with meat tenderizer and dry onion soup mix • In a small bowl, combine one can cream of mushroom soup and one to two cans of water (more water will make thinner gravy) • Pour over meat • Cover and cook at 350 degrees for 30 minutes • Reduce temperature to 250 degrees • Cook for 3 hours

time may need to be adjusted - check the meat after two hours

Kay and Janet Paschal

Guess which one is the tom boy?

glen's favorite soup supper

Glen was a picky eater when he married me. I changed that because I came from a family of seven children. When I first made this soup, he was sure he wouldn't like it, and only reluctantly tried it. It turned out to be one of his favorite soup suppers, and I became his favorite cook! I always made fried cornbread to go along with it.

Van Payne

3 quarts water
3 pounds ground beef
1 medium onion, chopped
1 tablespoon celery flakes or diced celery to taste
1 teaspoon dried parsley
½ teaspoon garlic powder
6 large potatoes, peeled and cubed
salt and pepper to taste

In a large stock pot, bring water to a boil • Crumble ground beef into the water • As meat begins to cook, continue to break apart into small pieces • Add onions, parsley, celery or celery flakes, garlic salt, salt and pepper • When meat is cooked thoroughly, the grease will rise to the top of the soup mixture • Remove as much grease as possible • Add potatoes and cook until tender • Serve with baked or fried cornbread

GLEN PAYNE

Glen Payne boating as a young boy

country fried steak meal

I laugh when I think about it. When I was a teenager, my mom would often cook country fried steak, potatoes, gravy and cornbread. I would complain about eating the same thing every week. "Not again!" still rings in Mama's ears today! However, when I started traveling full-time and after eating burgers and fries every day, I'd call home and beg Mama to fix me country fried steak, potatoes, gravy and cornbread! She'd often laugh and remind me of my previous ingratitude toward such a satisfying meal.

In our family, country fried steak goes back generations. My grandmother Tench was famous for her version of this dish. Being one of eight children, Mama remembers always having an appreciation and anticipation for Sunday dinner at home featuring her mom's country fried steak. For Mama, Sunday dinner and country fried steak go together like a fork and knife.

Over the years, I've discovered my own way of preparing country fried steak – the same as Mama and Grandma Tench did – adding a few new ingredients here and there. I grew up with lard and butter flowing through my veins, but a few years ago I ran across a recipe that works for my family, and they just LOVE it.

4 cubed steaks
2 cups flour
salt and pepper
5 large potatoes
1 pound bag fresh carrots
1 package onion soup mix
1 cup water

Pour flour into a resealable bag • Salt and pepper cubed steak • Put steak into resealable bag with flour and shake well until steak is well coated with flour • Pre-heat 3 to 4 tablespoons oil in skillet • Place meat in skillet and lightly brown on each side (discard remaining flour) • Preheat oven to 400 degrees • Peel potatoes and carrots • Cut into small chunks and place in a casserole dish • Lightly salt and pepper • Place browned cubed steaks over the top of potatoes and carrots • Sprinkle dry onion soup mix over the meat, potatoes and carrots • Pour in water • Cover with aluminum foil • Bake at 400 degrees for 1 hour or until potatoes and carrots are tender

Karen Peck (middle) with family

KAREN PECK

penrod's favorite orange caramel chicken

After Angie Penrod had served this family favorite a couple of times, the Penrod clan decided it definitely needed a little extra sauce on the side. But this special sauce was so delicious that the family soon began to drizzle it over rice, corn and any other vegetables served with the chicken. Not a morsel was left on their plates as they scraped up every last drop of the orange, buttery liquid candy with their bread or rolls! Angie says this is "an orange caramel casserole entrée and dessert all in one!"

4-6 boneless, skinless chicken breasts
¾ cup orange juice
¼ cup sugar
¼ cup butter

Combine orange juice, sugar and butter in a saucepan and simmer for 15 minutes or until thick • Preheat oven or grill • Bake at 350 degrees for 45 minutes or grill chicken, basting with orange caramel sauce every 15 minutes until done

The Penrod family

GUY PENROD

ugly pasta

People frequently ask, "How do you feed a family the size of yours?" Amazingly enough, we do eat at home most of the time and have turned to very large pans and "industrialized size" bowls. In the winter, we eat a lot of soup and homemade bread.

In the summer, we eat lots of pasta meals with a grilled meat or fish on the side. We eat a lot of whole foods – just the way God made 'em, and for health and convenience, we have a lot of baked potatoes, raw or steamed veggies, fresh bananas, watermelon, etc.

I line the front walk with cherry tomato plants and bush beans. One of my favorite summertime sights is the little fingers searching the plants for beans or plucking a handful of tomatoes from the vine as they walk by and popping them into their mouths.

We have an herb garden in the back yard by the kitchen. The basil does really well there, so each year I plant a little more so there is plenty to make pesto sauce. I especially love to feed pesto to the family because it's an "uncooked" green that's grown right in our garden. It's a quick meal, too. It can go from garden to table within 30 minutes! We call it ugly pasta because it is green and truly the ugliest food I feed them.

1 cup olive oil
fresh garlic to taste (about three or four cloves)
1 cup grated fresh parmesan cheese
1 cup pine nuts (or any nut you have on hand)
fresh basil leaves
3-4 pounds multi-grain pasta

Boil water in large stock pot and cook as directed • Meanwhile, blend all ingredients except basil in blender until smooth • Pack in the fresh basil leaves until blender reaches capacity • Blend until smooth • Spread sauce over three to four pounds of hot multi-grain pasta

A family meal at the Penrod home

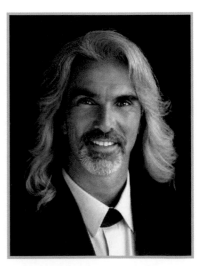

GUY PENROD

Someone asked me once, "How do you lose weight?" I replied in my normal sarcastic wit, "I have a tape worm." The kind elderly lady's countenance dropped as she said, "Oh, I'm so sorry. My niece had one and battled it for years. I will pray for you." I quickly replied in horror, "Please don't pray for me...I mean pray for me but not about my worm...I mean I don't have a tape worm — I was just kidding." She smirked as she walked away.

The truth is I always battle weight because of the great cooks in my family. I grew up eating Texas-style: chicken-fried steak, barbecued brisket, tex-mex, chocolate pie, sausage gravy and biscuits, and of course, my favorite "Five-Flavor Cake." We still have it at every family gathering. Mom makes three or four when we all get together. The recipe has just the right amount of sweetness and we can't get enough of it.

This recipe was handed down from my great-grandmother, Callie, in east central Texas. As a matter of fact we named our oldest daughter after her. Years ago she was curious about the woman from whom she inherited her name, so she sat down beside my grandfather and asked, "Grandpa, what was your mother like?"

"She was mean," he replied without a pause. Appalled, my mom quickly interrupted, "Daddy!" "Well, do you want the truth or something made up?" At this age he pretty much spoke his mind. "She was a hard worker. She was a great cook. She always loved us. But she was mean!" I leaned over to my daughter and said, "See honey, that's good stock you come from."

Enjoy the cake!

DAVID PHELPS

The Phelps family

five flavor cake

½ cup shortening
2 sticks butter or margarine
3 cups sugar
5 eggs, well beaten
1 teaspoon baking powder
3 cups flour
1 cup milk
1 teaspoon coconut flavor
1 teaspoon rum flavor
1 teaspoon butter flavor
1 teaspoon lemon flavor
1 teaspoon vanilla

Preheat oven to 325 degrees • Grease 10 inch tube or bundt cake pan well • In a large mixing bowl, cream butter, shortening and sugar until light and fluffy • Add well beaten eggs • In another mixing bowl, combine flour and baking powder • Add to creamed mixture alternately with milk • Stir in flavoring • Spoon into prepared cake pan • Bake at 325 degrees for 45-60 minutes, or until done

gazpacho

The Phelps family loves fresh vegetables, and when the tomatoes start producing, my mom, Mary Ella, makes up a double batch of gazpacho.

One day I came in from school and was getting some gazpacho for my after-school snack. Mom kept the gazpacho in a large Tupperware® bowl, one of those that had a circle in the center to help seal the lid. When I went to close the bowl, I punched the circle with my fist just as my mom walked into the kitchen. Gazpacho went everywhere – it was like an explosion – on the ceiling, the counter, the stove, and all over me. I looked at her, trying to decide if I should run away from home or start begging for mercy. All of a sudden, we both broke out giggling and then laughing until we cried.

We still love gazpacho, but make sure to store it in a jar that has a screw top lid! Also, Mom repainted the ceiling.

1 medium cucumber, peeled and quartered
1 medium green pepper, cored and quartered
1 small onion, peeled and quartered
2 sprigs parsley
1 clove garlic
6-7 ripe tomatoes, peeled and quartered
1 cup chilled tomato juice
3 tablespoons red wine vinegar
1 teaspoon salt
$\frac{1}{8}$ teaspoon pepper
dash tabasco

In a food processor, pulse the cucumber, green pepper, onion, parsley and garlic • Add tomatoes and remaining ingredients and pulse a bit more • Transfer mixture to a large bowl, cover and chill • Garnish with avocados, croutons or fresh parsley

DAVID PHELPS

David in high school

A strict teacher from our small town schoolhouse pronounced me, "Sick enough to go home," which translated to me, "I must be next door to dying." She was military ridged, and you had to be hospital sick to be released from her class.

Within moments my Uncle Donald came to fetch me in his work van with side panels boldly declaring, "That's What I Said...Bunny Bread!" He carried me out of school and gently placed me in the tiny buddy seat perched up front.

To my surprise, instead of driving me to my Grandma's house as usual, he pulled into the driveway of our tiny house trailer and grinned, "Your mom and dad got home a day early from the road!" On cue my tall lanky dad bolted out the door, rushed to the van, swooped me into his arms and with a quick thanks to Uncle Donald, cradled me into the house.

I got the first delicious whiff of their wafting aroma long before he reached the door handle...mom's peanut butter cookies! There she was, the most beautiful mom in the world sporting my favorite red housecoat, fragrant with First Lady

Cologne and dimples flashing! Quicker than you can say, "Florence Nightingale," mom dressed me in a cozy flannel gown, massaged a generous dollop of Vick's® vapor rub on my upper chest and cocooned me tightly in a colorful patchwork quilt.

Laughing over silly road stories, sipping hot chocolate with marshmallows and devouring warm peanut butter cookies...healing heaven!

Reba's mother, Dottie Rambo

REBA RAMBO MCGUIRE

peanut butter cookies

½ cup butter
½ cup peanut butter
½ cup sugar
½ cup brown sugar
1 egg
½ teaspoon vanilla
1 ¼ cups flour
¾ teaspoon soda
¼ teaspoon salt
powdered sugar

Preheat oven to 325 degrees • Grease
cookie sheet • In a bowl, cream
together butter, peanut butter, sugars,
egg and vanilla; mix well • Add dry
ingredients into butter mixture • Shape
into one inch balls and place on cookie
sheet • With a fork, press deeply across
top of each cookie in a cross pattern •
Sprinkle with powdered sugar • Bake
at 325 degrees for 10-12 minutes •
Yields 30 cookies

Growing up in Washington, DC, in a family with lots of siblings and both parents from the south, you better believe that there was food, and lots of it! Especially foods directly related to the south like collard greens, fatback, black-eyed peas, pan-fried chicken, corn on the cob and one of my all time favorite dishes – potato salad – Mmm Mmm good!! I'm not just talking about any ol' potato salad, I'm talking about that little country girl (Maxine Tait) that haled from Wadesboro, NC who met my daddy (Nathel J. Tait) from Mobile, AL and became my incredible, personal, southern "Chef Momma" kind of potato salad. The kind that will make you want to slap your momma three generations back! – THAT KIND OF POTATO SALAD! It's the kind that melts in your mouth and will have you salivating for more before your plate is empty! It seemed to go with just about everything we ate, but of course, Momma couldn't make it everyday. Married with seven children, working a full-time job and all, when on earth would she have that kind of time?

Her potato salad is probably one of the reasons that I love picnics and cookouts even now. I can't recall ever having a picnic or cookout, whether we were hosting or invited guests to someone else's gathering, that momma didn't serve up her "taste-bud-dancing" potato salad. I can still smell the flame broiled burgers, hot dogs, and chicken cooking on the grill. I can hear the sound of the softball hitting the bat and the screams and cheers of excitement because one of my siblings finally got off home base.

We enjoyed and endured all of this hooplah and family fun while trying desperately to bide our time until the food was ready. Sometimes it seemed as if the smoke from the grill had only one path it traveled that day – straight to our noses – awakening every taste bud that lay dormant. Taunting and tantalizing our hungry little bellies with the vague promise that we would be nourished and all would be well. But what seemed to us an eternity and even longer perhaps, vanished when without warning the "call" came. "COME AND GET IT, FOOD'S READY!" And like missiles being launched into outer space, we raced to the picnic table leaving behind bats, balls, gloves, incomplete scores and sometimes each other.

Did somebody say "picnic?"

Lynda and her husband, Michael

mashed potato salad

5 pound bag idaho® potatoes, peeled
  and cut into ½ inch cubes
7-8 large eggs, hard-boiled, peeled,
  chopped and cooled
1 tablespoon salt

sauce
2 ½ cups real mayonnaise
1 tablespoon yellow mustard
½ tablespoon sugar, level
1 tablespoon celery seed
1 teaspoon sweet relish juice
½ teaspoon salt
½ teaspoon lemon juice
1 teaspoon paprika (optional)

Cut potatoes into ½ inch cubes • Rinse
with cold water • Place potatoes in
large pot and cover with cold water •
Add one tablespoon salt • Bring
potatoes to boil over high heat •
Continue to boil on high until potatoes
are very tender and falling apart •
Drain and allow to cool for 15 minutes •
Place cooled potatoes in large mixing
bowl • Add eggs and stir • Set aside

For sauce, in a medium mixing bowl
combine mayonnaise, yellow mustard,
sugar, celery seed, relish juice, salt, and
lemon juice • Mix thoroughly • Add
sauce to potato and egg mixture • Stir
until evenly mixed and salt to taste •
Place in casserole dish and garnish
with paprika • Serve warm or
refrigerate for three to four hours

mom's meatloaf

My mom's meatloaf has always been one of my favorite meals. I never tried making it myself until a few years ago. I was about nine months pregnant and the idea of that meatloaf was making my mouth water. I decided to make mom's recipe myself and as it cooked, it smelled just like hers.

I never got the chance to taste it, however, because no sooner had I fixed Greg's plate, I went into labor. I didn't get to eat one bite, but when we came home from the hospital, the first meal my mom made for us was her meatloaf. It is my favorite dish for some very special reasons!

2 pounds lean ground beef
1 small onion diced
1 egg
dash of salt and pepper
1 (10.5 ounce) can tomato soup

In a large bowl, mix together beef, onion, egg, salt and pepper • Form mixture into a loaf in a shallow pan or iron skillet • Pour tomato soup on top of the loaf • Bake for one hour at 350 degrees • Serve with your favorite veggies

CHARLOTTE RITCHIE

Charlotte on the carousel with her mother

fluffy tapioca pudding

The term "comfort food" definitely comes to mind when I think about this recipe. My mom made several wonderful desserts, but my favorite has always been Fluffy Tapioca Pudding. About a year after mom passed away, I wanted to surprise my dad, brothers and the rest of our family with a nice dinner. For dessert, I made Mom's pudding. It brought back so many memories and was a comfort to us all. We could just see ourselves sitting around the table, laughing with Mom and enjoying a great meal together.

I think you'll love this pudding!

2 cups milk
1 egg white
1 egg yolk
6 tablespoons sugar, divided
1 teaspoon vanilla
3 tablespoons minute tapioca

Beat egg white in a medium bowl with mixer on high until foamy • Gradually add three tablespoons sugar, beating until soft peaks form • Mix tapioca, remaining sugar, milk and egg yolk in a medium saucepan • Let stand five minutes • Cook on medium heat, stirring constantly until mixture comes to full boil • Remove from heat • Quickly stir in egg white mixture until well blended • Stir in vanilla • Let cool for about 20 minutes and stir • Serve warm or chilled

CHARLOTTE RITCHIE

Charlotte and
her mother

mom's indian stew

This recipe is one I created when my boys were just little guys. There were times when I wanted to do something special for them. I would create yummy things to eat, especially when money was tight and we couldn't afford to drive through a fast-food restaurant for the "proverbial bribe." The guys always loved for me to make sloppy joes, but that can get a bit boring every other day, so I created something I called "Indian Stew." It was an instant hit and became a tradition. When I would ask the boys what they would like for me to cook for a special occasion – you guessed it – Indian Stew.

They still love this simple dish today. It makes me think of how God can take such little things in our lives and make very big blessings out of them. Damon and Justin would rather have Mom's "Indian Stew" than a ten course meal, and that is a precious gem to me. I hope this dish will be a blessing to others, too.

1 ½ to 2 pounds lean ground beef
1 (17 ounce) can whole kernel corn, drained
1 (15.5 ounce) can pinto beans, drained
1 medium onion, chopped
2 tablespoons onion powder
2 tablespoons seasoning salt
1 teaspoon salt
1 teaspoon red pepper (optional)
1 ½ tablespoons lemon pepper
1 ½ teaspoons pepper
1 (6 ounce) can tomato paste
½ cup ketchup

Cook ground beef until done, drain off excess grease • Add onions and all seasonings to meat and cook until onions are clear • Add tomato paste and mix, then add beans and corn • Stir well, and add in ketchup • If needed, add ¼ to ½ cup water for desired consistency • Simmer for 30 to 45 minutes on low heat to bring out full flavor

LuLu with her boys, Justin and Damon

LULU ROMAN

cheesy chicken

This recipe was given to me by my sister. She cooked my group a wonderful meal, and I enjoyed it so much that I asked for the recipe.

Just as our bodies need food everyday, so our soul needs food from the Word, prayer and good gospel music. We are always blessed when we have the opportunity to hear a good sermon on a Sunday morning – that's food for our soul.

I am so thankful for having been raised in a Christian home by Godly parents and being able to sing His Gospel for all these years proclaiming Him King of Kings and LORD of LORDS.

Psalm 37:4 "Delight thyself also in the LORD, and He shall give thee the desires of thine heart."

1 (10 ounce) can cream of chicken soup
1 soup can of milk
½ teaspoon salt
1 cup cooked chicken, chopped
1 cup instant rice
1 cup shredded cheddar cheese

In a large saucepan, combine soup, milk, salt, chicken and rice • Bring to a boil stirring occasionally • Remove from heat and let set for 10 minutes covered • Preheat oven to 350 degrees • Grease a 1 ½ quart dish • Place ½ cup of grated cheese, then layer the chicken mixture into the dish • Top with the remaining ½ cup cheese • Bake at 350 degrees for 25 minutes • Serve with salad or green vegetable

Original Sego group:
James, Naomi,
W.R. and Lamar

Naomi and The Segos

I often associate eating with a happening in my life, and this is how I met my wonderful late husband, Vernon Reader. I was living in the small town of White House, Tennessee, and we had to drive to Goodlettsville to do any kind of shopping. I decided before shopping I would get something to eat, so I went to Morrison's Cafeteria. On my way to find a table, some friends, Randy and Mary Byrd, saw me and invited me to their table. Vernon Reader was having lunch with them that day. He was in revival at the Hendersonville Church of God, and they were singing at the revival. That was our first encounter, and when I went to the revival one night, he asked me if I would go out with him. Needless to say, that day changed my life.

We had 15 wonderful years together. I truly believe the Lord directed my steps that day, and He had sent Vernon all the way from Texas to Tennessee, I believe just for me. Vernon passed away October 16, 1998. I know he is with the Lord, the One he preached and sung about. We will be together again with our loved ones, and "What a day, glorious day that will be."

NAOMI SEGO READER

low fat carrot cake

cake
4 cups carrots, grated and loosely packed
4 cups sugar
1 can (8 ounce) crushed pineapple
1 cup prune puree (recipe below)
4 large egg whites
2 teaspoons vanilla
2 cups flour
2 teaspoons baking soda
2 teaspoons cinnamon
½ teaspoon salt
½ cup shredded or flaked coconut

prune puree
1 ⅓ cups prunes, pitted
6 tablespoons water

Preheat oven to 375 degrees • Grease 9 x 13 baking pan • In a large bowl, combine carrots, sugar, pineapple, prune puree, egg whites and vanilla • Stir to blend thoroughly • Add remaining ingredients except coconut and mix completely • Gently stir in coconut • Spread batter in prepared pan and bake for 45 minutes or until tooth pick inserted into center comes out clean • Cool on rack • Cut into 3 x 3 ½ inch pieces • Makes 12 servings

For the prune puree combine pitted prunes and six tablespoons water in a food processor • Pulse on and off until prunes are finely chopped • Makes one cup

Sego Brothers and Naomi

chocolate brownie cobbler

Growing up in a Christian family, we were obviously very familiar with Sunday evening socials. Every Sunday night after church, we would gather around a table, a piano, and often a Bible, for what we would call "after-glows" (I never have understood exactly what that meant, or where it came from, but it's what we called it).

Our family did not have the most money or the biggest house, but in my opinion, we did have the best mom, greatest memories and warmest – and most delicious – Chocolate Brownie Cobbler. It became a tradition that every time folks would gather in our family room, Mom would serve chocolate brownie cobbler, ice cream and love.

Our home was used more than any other for Sunday evenings, and people preferred it that way. I'm not sure what brought them back week after week – the cobbler, ice cream or the love – probably all three! Mom is now famous for her recipe. She has passed it on to me, and so I pass it on to you.

STAN SHERIDAN

2 cups sugar
1 ½ cups self-rising flour
3 eggs
1 teaspoon vanilla
½ cup cocoa
1 ½ sticks butter

Preheat oven to 325 degrees • Grease 9 x 13 inch glass baking dish • In a small mixing bowl, melt butter and stir in cocoa until smooth; set aside • In medium size mixing bowl, beat eggs until creamy • Add sugar, cocoa and butter to egg mixture • Gradually add flour and stir • Mix by hand, do not use blender • Pour into glass pan • Bake at 325 degrees for 25 minutes • Serve with ice cream

The Sheridan family

HENRY AND HAZEL SLAUGHTER

Henry and I joined the Weatherford Quartet in Akron, Ohio in late 1957. Armond's wife Clara Morales and I quickly became friends. She and Armond invited us for dinner and she served tacos which were a big hit with us. Later, when she was expecting their second child, I stayed with her while Henry and Armond were away on a trip. Clara had been craving some homemade "California Mexican" food. Her mother sent her the necessary masa harina, Spanish for "dough flour" for the meal. I watched her prepare the tortillas. I decided I had to learn how to do this for my own family. After many attempts to make them the proper shape and size, I finally mastered it and making tortillas became a routine. I've served them at our family table and to many others in the Weatherford and Cathedral of Tomorrow church staff. Everywhere we have lived since then, I have introduced these most loved dishes and then taught others to make them. They are still a lunch or dinner special at our home.

That first Mexican cooking lesson was more than 50 years ago. It's easy, fun, and oh, so delightful! I never had anyone turn them down when I served them for the first time, and they always come back for more. Thank you, Clara.

hazel's handmade tortillas

2 cups masa harina (or corn masa flour)
1 cup hot water, not boiling
canola oil, several tablespoons

enchiladas
1 (12 ounce) can evaporated milk
1 (14.5 ounce) can chopped tomatoes with green chilies
1 (10.5 ounce) can cream of mushroom soup
1 (10.5 ounce) can cream of chicken soup
1 (10 ounce) can enchilada sauce
1 rotisserie chicken; pull meat off bones
shredded cheese to taste

tacos
ground beef
onion powder (dash)
cumin (dash)

toppings
lettuce, chopped
tomato, chopped
onion, chopped
grated cheese

tortillas
In a large bowl, mix water and masa until dough holds shape • Roll dough into small balls (slightly larger than an egg) • Place one ball of dough onto a tea towel and cover with a square of plastic cut from a freezer bag • Roll ball of dough out smoothly, making sure it retains an even thickness • Heat one tablespoon of canola oil in a hot skillet and fry tortilla for a few seconds on each side until light brown and crispy, but soft • Stack between

Henry and Hazel

~ continued ~

paper towels to absorb excess oil •
Repeat steps with remaining dough

enchiladas
Preheat oven to 350 degrees •
In a bowl, combine first five
ingredients and mix well • Add
chicken to sauce • Cover homemade
tortillas with a layer of sauce and
a layer of cheese • Repeat for
each enchilada and bake at 350
degrees for 45 minutes

tacos
In a skillet, brown ground beef
with onion powder and cumin •
Discard excess grease • Add beans
and simmer for 5-10 minutes • Serve
beef mixture in tortillas with toppings

Lillie Knauls tells a story to
James Blackwood and Gloria Gaither.

Bill and Gloria Gaither sharing
a laugh with Mark Lowry

Russ Taff, Frank Mills, Doug Anderson and
Ernie Haase at a ranch steakhouse in Arizona

The Speer sisters, Mary Tom and Rosa Nell,
at the *Homcoming Picnic* taping

Gloria and Bill Gaither at the
Count Your Blessings taping

Doug Oldham in the banquet line at
the Gaither complex for a taping

Gathering around the Goodman family table

Deep conversation at a favorite
Alaskan fish and chips restaurant

perfectly marinated pork chops

My mother was a home economics teacher, nutritionist and an incredible cook. We always had wonderful meals and cooking really was my mother's special gift. She loved sharing her warm southern hospitality with everyone, and part of that kindness was preparing meals and sharing them with others. She found joy in preparing dishes for a family who lost a loved one or a young couple who had just moved into a new home in the neighborhood. On occasion, she would invite the widows from church over for a brunch just to lift their spirits. She took so much delight in cooking for friends and family, and everyone enjoyed sampling her latest creation!

One of my very favorite dishes is my mother's marinated pork chops. It was the food of choice each year for my "birthday dinner." Even when I was older, I couldn't wait to come home from college to this wonderful meal. My mom created the sauce, and Daddy did the grilling. The end result was perfectly marinated pork chops!

½ cup soy sauce
¼ cup light brown sugar
2 shakes of garlic powder
¼ teaspoon ginger
¼ cup water
extra-thick cut loin chops (cut to approximately ½ inch)

In a bowl, combine soy sauce, brown sugar, ginger, water and two dashes of garlic powder • Pour marinade into resealable bag or shallow dish • Add pork and marinate in refrigerator for at least 8 hours, flipping occasionally • Grill, fry or bake pork chops to desired doneness

One other way we modified this over the years: My daddy says (to make them even tastier) after placing them on the grill, it is important to keep pouring the remainder of the sauce over the chops while grilling to keep them moist. Mom always served baked beans, a green bean casserole, a cold gelatin salad and hot, homemade rolls with the pork chops to create my favorite meal!

Ladye Love's mother, Yvonne

yvonne's famous breakfast steaks

I cook like a true southerner – a little of this, a dash of that. Who needs a measuring cup? I learned from the best how to eyeball the simplest of ingredients to create the tastiest of meals. My mom's breakfast steaks are famous in my family. Saturday mornings are the best times for our breakfast spread; complete with eggs, gravy and biscuits. Reggie and I want our son, Bret, to have as many warm memories of home as we have had.

top round steaks – cut very thinly
flour
pepper
seasoning salt or salt
vegetable oil

In a resealable bag, lightly flour, salt and pepper steaks, toss to ensure flour mixture coats both sides of steaks • Fry steaks in oil in a cast iron skillet until done • Make gravy with drippings and serve with hot biscuits or eggs

REGGIE AND LADYE LOVE SMITH

Ladye Love and her son, Bret

My mother always cooked this breakfast roll when I had friends over, especially when we all were in high school and then later when we would come home from college. We all just loved it!

A friend recently told me she was wishing for a taste of the breakfast roll my mother used to make when she spent the night those many years ago.

This recipe sounds difficult, but it's really easy and will look like you spent hours in the kitchen, and it is so nice to wake up to the marvelous smell as it is baking!

breakfast jam loaf

loaf
1 package yeast
1 egg
½ cup warm water
1 tablespoon sugar
2 ½ cups bisquick® mix

filling
8 ounce cream cheese
½ cup sugar
1 tablespoon lemon juice – or more to taste
blackberry jam

Spray 9 x 13 inch baking sheet with cooking spray • Dissolve yeast in warm water • Combine bisquick,® beaten egg and 1 tablespoon sugar • Add to yeast mixture and stir 20 strokes • Spread on a baking sheet • Combine filling ingredients and spread down the center of crust • Fold each side over to meet in the middle • Bake at 350 degrees for about 20 minutes • Add your favorite jam or jelly down the middle where the crust edges meet, and bake an additional 5 minutes • As an alternative presentation, cut 1 inch wide strips about three inches long on both sides; leaving the three-inch center uncut • Continue with jam as directed above • You can make this the night before and refrigerate until ready to bake

Ladye Love and Reggie at home

faye's ice cream

I'm sure every family has favorite foods that they feel have to be served at every special event. My family thinks my homemade ice cream should be the dessert for every birthday celebration and any other time they can get me to make it.

When our youngest son Brian was in college, we decided to have some of his friends over to the house for ice cream and cake. I bought the cake and it was beautiful. I had matching bowls and napkins and we were all set. I dished up the ice cream and not a sound was heard. Brian finally came over to me and asked in a soft voice, "Mom, what's wrong with it?" I tasted it and realized it had no sugar. I had forgotten a very important ingredient for ice cream.

They were all very gracious and a good time was had by all that day, but it is one birthday we will never forget. That was one of life's embarrassing moments for me.

If you decide to try this recipe, don't forget the sugar!

1 ½ cups sugar
4 eggs or egg substitute
1 (14 ounce) can sweetened condensed milk
1 (12 ounce) can evaporated milk
1 pint heavy cream
1 tablespoon vanilla
1 can pineapple, crushed
3 bananas, mashed
1 cup orange juice
½ gallon whole milk

In a large bowl, combine eggs and sugar; mix well • Add bananas to sugar mixture • Add remaining ingredients and stir well • Pour into gallon ice cream freezer • Add whole milk to fill freezer to capacity and freeze as directed

FAYE SPEER

Faye and
her son, Brian

My grandmother, Lucy Hayes, was the first person I remember making this recipe. She could make pies, cakes and fried chicken taste heavenly! My mother also made this recipe for me when I was a child, and now I enjoy making this recipe for my children.

grandma lucy's easy cinnamon rolls

biscuit dough
½ - ⅔ cup brown sugar
cinnamon to taste
butter, melted

Preheat oven to 350 degrees • Grease a 9 x 9 cake pan • Using your favorite biscuit dough recipe, place dough onto a flat surface • With a rolling pin, roll out dough into a rectangle, much thinner than an actual biscuit - about ½ inch to 1 inch in size • Spread a layer of brown sugar onto the dough • Sprinkle cinnamon over the brown sugar • Roll dough into a log shape, beginning with the long side • Slice to desired thickness • Place one biscuit in the middle of the pan and the remaining biscuits around it • Brush or dot rolls with butter • Bake at 350 degrees for 12-15 minutes or until golden brown

The Speers: Ann Downing, Faye Speer, Sherrill Neilson, Brock and Ben Speer

FAYE SPEER

TANYA GOODMAN SYKES

It was very exciting living in the house with my dad because we never knew who he would bring home for dinner. Thank goodness my mom was a good cook and a good sport because just about every day my dad would call from the office and say, "I've got some folks here who would love to have a home-cooked meal." Record company presidents, politicians, gospel singers, professional football players, evangelists, struggling song writers and hungry young band members were all seated around our table at one time or another. And, of course, there were always six or eight stray folks who couldn't get back home to share the holidays with their own families. They were all greeted with the same warmth and hospitality. Early on, I learned from my mom how to "go with the flow." Although she liked to keep a sparkling clean house and prepare well thought out meals, she didn't let it ruffle her feathers if it didn't work out that way. She would give the house what she called a "lick and a promise," add a few more carrots to the stew and welcome our guests with open arms. Guess what? No one ever complained! I've encountered many people over the years, some familiar and some long forgotten, who told me how much they enjoyed the time they spent in our home...and they always ask about the gracious lady who was their hostess.

Tanya Goodman Sykes with her mom, Billie Goodman, her youngest daughter, Aly, and her husband, Michael

billie goodman's chicken cacciatore

1 frying chicken, cut into pieces
garlic salt
pepper
1 cup flour
1 (28 ounce) can whole tomatoes
1 (16 ounce) can tomato sauce
1 tablespoon soy sauce
cooking oil

Wash chicken and leave slightly moist •
Generously season chicken with garlic
salt and pepper, then roll in flour • Add
enough cooking oil to cover the bottom
of an iron skillet and sauté chicken until
tender • Drain grease from the skillet •
Add tomatoes, tomato sauce, one can
of water and soy sauce • Cover and
simmer over low heat until mixture
thickens into sauce • Serve over rice or
angel hair pasta

rusty's homemade ice cream

Dad really came into his own as a "chef" when he got a gas grill for the patio. There was nothing he loved to do more than grill a juicy steak and whip up a freezer of homemade ice cream. Although these are traditionally summertime activities, I've seen my dad put on a coat to dash out in the freezing rain to turn his steak or to check on a freezer of ice cream. He fiddled around with the formula for years and finally got it just the way he wanted it. Occasionally he would toss in some sliced peaches or strawberries, but most folks liked it straight up. He gave me a copy of it in his own handwriting, and I have it framed and hanging in my kitchen. It's a creation that was as much a part of him as any song he ever wrote.

TANYA GOODMAN SYKES

½ pint whipping cream
1 cup sugar
6 eggs or egg substitute
¼ teaspoon salt
2 tablespoons vanilla extract
2 cans evaporated milk
1 (14 ounce) can sweetened condensed milk
additional milk

Combine whipping cream, sugar, eggs, salt and vanilla into a bowl and mix thoroughly • Pour mixture into ice cream freezer canister and add evaporated milk and sweetened condensed milk • Add regular milk until mixture reaches fill line • Start ice cream machine • Makes 1 gallon

Tanya and her Dad, Rusty

When I was a young girl, there was a huge white farm-style house with a pristine lawn and white picket fence just a few doors down from us. I was fascinated by it, and one spring day, I took it upon myself to meet the occupants. Peeking through the fence, I saw a gray-haired lady working in the flower bed and called out to her in the friendliest voice I could muster. She opened the gate, invited me in with a big grandmotherly hug, and we became instant pals. I spent many hours "helping" her with her yard work, and afterwards we'd retire to the squeaky, white glider on the porch. There she served up good old-fashioned conversation and an endless supply of icy lemonade in pink and blue aluminum tumblers. She had a large strawberry patch behind her house, and I earned lots of quarters picking berries every June. She was an excellent cook and would occasionally invite me into her kitchen to sample a fresh slice of pie. My very favorite was her chocolate pie, so one day I asked her for the recipe. Mom and I have been making it ever since, and it's a real hit with my girls, too. Looking back, I'm not sure how much Mrs. Welborn really needed my help, but I certainly needed her. She taught me a little about gardening, how to pick the perfect strawberry, and how to make the best chocolate pie in the world. But more than that, she invested her time in a little girl who didn't have a grandma close by.

TANYA GOODMAN SYKES

Tanya, as a young girl, around the time she worked for Mrs. Welborn

Tanya Goodman Sykes with Joy Gardner at the *Homecoming Picnic* taping

iron skillet chocolate pie

pie
1 baked pie shell
1 cup sugar
2 tablespoons flour
3 tablespoons cocoa
2 tablespoons butter
3 egg yolks (reserve whites
  for meringue)
1 cup milk
vanilla to taste

meringue
reserved egg whites
⅛ teaspoon cream of
  tartar
2 tablespoons sugar

Mix sugar, flour and cocoa in a small mixing bowl; mix well • Melt butter in an iron skillet over medium heat • Stir in sugar mixture • In a separate bowl, beat egg yolks, add milk and combine • Add the egg and milk mixture to the sugar mixture in the skillet a little at a time, stirring constantly • Cook slowly until thick • Add vanilla and allow to cool before pouring into a baked pie shell

For meringue, preheat oven to 400 degrees • Beat egg whites with hand mixer on high until stiff peaks form • Add cream of tartar and sugar • Top pie with meringue and bake for 8 minutes at 400 degrees or until golden brown • Allow pie to cool before serving

mama's chocolate gravy

Let the sugar rush begin! It's been said that it is the simple things that make life really worth living. You'll probably be a believer in that after trying chocolate gravy!

"I love chocolate gravy! A lot of people haven't heard of it, but I grew up with it. My mama still makes it. You stir it all up and pour it over your favorite biscuits, and it's really quite delicious!"

I grew up near Fresno, California, but the chocolate gravy recipe comes from my mother's southern heritage in Hot Springs, Arkansas. Chocolate gravy was always a big thing at our house on the weekends. Oh, man, you talk about a sugar rush! You speed up like crazy, and then you just crash.

I recall one time in the kitchen when I accidentally reversed the proportion of cocoa to sugar. It was a BIG mess!

Of course, even made right, it's not a bit good for you! I guess the biscuits aren't good for you either – at least not the way Mama makes 'em! If you've never had chocolate gravy, you gotta try it!

2 cups sugar
3 tablespoons flour
3 tablespoons cocoa
pinch of salt
1 ½-2 cups water

Combine all dry ingredients in a large mixing bowl, stirring thoroughly • While stirring, add water to desired consistency, mixing well with ingredients • Stir mixture over low heat in a medium size saucepan until mixture begins to simmer • Remove from heat and serve immediately

The Taff family

RUSS TAFF

nanno's pancakes

My mother-in-law Alexine has six children, eleven grandchildren and two great-grandchildren, and they stand united about their all-time favorite breakfast: Nanno's pancakes. As far back as anyone can remember, Nanno's delicious 'cakes have been made to order in all manner of forms – cats, turtles, dinosaurs, Christmas trees and bunnies. "I made them in different shapes for my own children," Alexine remembers. "It just continued on down through the grandchildren."

My girls, Maddie Rose and Charlotte, are possibly the biggest fans of Nanno's specialty. "I've tasted some really good pancakes in my day," Maddie Rose says seriously, "but not like these." Charlotte chimes in, "They always make me really happy. I feel sad for people who just have round pancakes."

Though pancake batter is a tricky medium, Nanno is never afraid to try new things. She even figured out how to spell words, pouring the batter into backward letters that become readable when they were turned over.

But it's mostly about making memories, and Nanno has certainly succeeded in doing that. "One time she spelled out 'I love you,' in pancakes, Charlotte says. "That was the best."

2 cups all-purpose flour
5 teaspoons baking powder
pinch of salt
1 tablespoon sugar
2 eggs
2 cups milk
¼ cup oil

In a bowl, mix flour with baking powder, salt and sugar • In another bowl, beat eggs, add milk and stir in the oil • Add to flour mixture • Beat by hand or with a small hand mixer until perfectly smooth • Heat griddle moderately and oil lightly by rubbing a paper towel dipped in oil across the surface • Gently add a small amount of batter to preheated skillet • Cook and flip • Serve with syrup and butter

Nanno making pancakes

pat and dolly's fresh coconut cake

This cake is a long-standing tradition at our house. My mother has made it for years for our Christmas gatherings. It usually takes her the better part of an afternoon to create this incredible dessert. (Well worth it from my end of the fork!)

When I was growing up, our church family was very close. One of the ladies in our little congregation was somewhat of a mentor to my mom. Dolly was a sweet lady and an awesome cook. Many years ago, she gave my mom her recipe for fresh coconut cake. My mom has made it ever since. I remember my mom buying a real coconut and taking a hammer to it to extract its milk and sweet meat for this delicacy. Thank goodness it comes in a package now!

Many people have their own special coconut cake recipe, but this is my all-time favorite. Is it that good? Of course, it is! Or it could be that I can just taste the love my mom puts in it? I hope you enjoy.

cake
2 eggs
2 cups sugar
2 ½ cups self-rising flour, sifted
½ cup shortening
2 cups buttermilk
1 teaspoon baking soda
1 teaspoon vanilla or ½ teaspoon coconut flavoring and ½ teaspoon vanilla
1 (6 ounce) package frozen coconut or small bag (8 ounces) dry sweetened coconut – more if you would like to add coconut to the cake batter

icing
1 cup sugar
½ cup white corn syrup
½ cup water
½ cup miniature marshmallows
3 egg whites

cake
Preheat oven to 350 degrees. Grease two 9 inch cake pans • In a large bowl, cream shortening and sugar • Beat eggs into the sugar mixture one at a time • In another bowl, sift dry ingredients together • Slowly add dry ingredients to sugar mixture while alternating with buttermilk until all is combined • Add vanilla and fold in optional coconut • Gently pour cake mixture into prepared cake pans • Bake at 350 degrees

Debra as a little girl

⌒ continued ⌒

for 30 minutes or until toothpick inserted in center comes out clean • Cool and remove from pans • Let layers cool before icing

icing
In a saucepan, create a simple syrup by mixing sugar, corn syrup and water until a thread will spin six to eight inches long • Add marshmallows and stir until melted • In a separate bowl, beat three egg whites until stiff • When syrup is ready, add to beaten egg whites, beating constantly with mixer until stiff peaks form

assembly of cake
Cover the first layer with cooled icing • Top with second layer • Cover sides and top of cake with remaining icing • Coat top and sides of cake in coconut

The first words my mother-in-law ever spoke to me were "I hate men, and I hate musicians!" You gotta love that. This is a mother-in-law story; one of those memorable ever endearing mother-in-law stories. I love Evelyn, that's her name. She is also my best friend. Evelyn is a first generation Lebanese American. Her parents came over on a boat from Lebanon with their faith, their love, a dream and this wonderful food.

The first time Evelyn served me Lebanese food, it came to the table in many strange colors and textures. There was hummus beige christened in olive oil gold, tabouleh green and grain, and pita bread white and shades of brown. Then came this platter of steaming leafy green things – dark green slippery things. I was to learn soon enough that these were grape leaf rolls (and perhaps I was to learn another of life's less subtle lessons).

Anyway, almost at once the familiar hum at the table stopped, and an awkward hush, this deathlike stillness, spread as I actually heard myself say (this actually came out of me), "I'm not eating that." (Oops!) All eyes turned to her, and with

that typical mother-in-law élan, Evelyn took my jaw in one hand and a grape leaf roll in the other and "stuffed" it into my mouth. I could offer but little resistance as she was too quick and too skillful at this.

Years later, perhaps from some deep psychological imprint of such a moment, I now love – no I crave – grape leaf rolls, and I've learned to make them myself. A memory in every bite.

David Teems' mother-in-law, Evelyn

DAVID TEEMS

stuffed grape leaf rolls

100 grape leaves
1 cup rice (uncooked)
1 ½ pounds lamb (or ground beef),
  coarsely ground
Salt, pepper, cinnamon, allspice to taste
2 lemons

Wash grape leaves and pour boiling water over leaves to soften • Wash and drain rice • Mix rice, lamb, spices and juice of one lemon • Place about one tablespoon of meat mixture on the veined side of each grape leaf • Spread across in a line, turn in the side ends and roll up completely • It will look like a green egg roll • Roll a bit loosely • Line bottom of three quart sauce pan or soup pot with 3 or 4 grape leaves • Place rolled grape leaves evenly in a row • Lay another row going the opposite direction • Continue in layers until all grape rolls are used • Place an inverted plate on top to hold down rolls • Add water to cover plate • Bring to boil • Reduce to low heat and cook 20-30 minutes • Add juice of one lemon 5 minutes before removing from heat • Serve with plain yogurt

swedish coffee cake

Swedish Coffee Cake has been a family favorite recipe for many years. Our four children would not want a holiday to pass without this delicious confection. Therefore, our two daughters-in-law have also learned to bake it.

We had a large family of seven children, and when times were difficult, Mother tried to help Dad every way she could. During the depression, she would bake this coffee cake, and we children would go door to door selling it. Many Christmas treats were bought with this money even though she only sold it for 10¢ a loaf. Mother always felt that was how the Lord provided as He did many times.

Submitted before Alden's death in 2007

cake
1 quart milk
2 packages yeast
1 cup sugar
1 tablespoon salt
⅓ cup shortening
1 ½ cups raisins
6 to 8 cups flour
cinnamon

icing
3 cups sifted powdered
  sugar
1 teaspoon butter
evaporated milk

Place yeast in a mixing bowl with a little warm water to dissolve • Put milk and shortening in a sauce pan and heat slowly only until shortening melts • Pour into bowl with yeast, then add sugar, salt, raisins and stir • Add flour one cup at a time until a soft mixture is formed, making sure not to get it too dry • Cover and allow to rise until double in size • Place dough onto floured cloth and divide into four parts • Roll out each section to the length of your bread pans and sprinkle with cinnamon • Roll up dough and insert into greased bread pans, tucking the ends • Again, allow to rise to double in size • Preheat oven to 375 degrees • Bake for 20 minutes or until brown • Cool completely and top with icing • Makes 4 loaves

icing
In a large bowl, combine sugar and butter • Add evaporated milk and beat to desired consistency • Spread on top of coffee cake

Betty and Alden Toney

ma goble's chicken and dumplings

My mother was a good ol' fashioned cook. She cooked the kind of food that was filling and delicious. Although money was scarce, Mother always had plenty to eat. Whatever it was, it was always good and there was more than enough. She would always say, "I want to have a little left over." That way she knew we would all have enough.

Every time I fix chicken and dumplings, I think of my sweet mother. Meal time at our house was a family affair, everyone at the table at the same time. Mother believed that dinner or supper should be a happy, enjoyable time, and our meal time was always very pleasant.

Our family could always rely on three things at meal time: it was going to be delicious, it was going to be a happy time, and there was always plenty.

LILY FERN WEATHERFORD

1 stewing hen or fryer
2 cups buttermilk
1 teaspoon salt
½ level teaspoon baking soda
3 to 4 cups flour
1 quart half and half
3 teaspoons flour
water to cover chicken

In a large pot cover chicken with water • Add salt and pepper to taste • Cook until tender, 45 minutes to an hour • When chicken is tender, remove from broth and allow to cool • Skin and debone chicken setting the meat aside

To make dumplings, pour buttermilk into a large bowl • Add baking soda and salt • Stir 3-4 cups of flour into buttermilk mixture to make a very soft dough • Dumpling mix should be a little thinner than biscuit dough so that it will drop from a spoon • In a large saucepan, bring remaining broth to a boil • Drop dumplings into broth stirring occasionally to keep dumplings from sticking • After all dumplings have been placed in the pot, dissolve three teaspoons of flour in water, ¼ cup of cold water and add back into the dumplings to thicken • Pour one quart half and half over broth and

Lily's mother, Ma Goble

The Weatherfords: (back row) Earl Weatherford, George Younce, Lily Fern Weatherford, (front) Danny Koker and Les Roberson

⁓ continued ⁓

dumplings • Continue cooking
until mixture begins to bubble
around the edges • Return
chicken pieces to pot • Simmer
15 to 20 minutes • Serves 6

old-fashioned strawberry pudding

Anytime we would visit Mom's parents, "MaMa" and "PaPa," or they would come to our house, there would always be some sweet treat MaMa had made for us to enjoy. One such confection was Strawberry Pudding, and I was "evermore excited" when this is what she had made for us! Through the years, this dessert became associated with birthdays, Thanksgiving and Christmas feasts. My mom has carried on this wonderful tradition, perfecting her own version of the family recipe. I have eaten many a banana pudding at friend's homes and church homecomings, but my favorite is its close relative, the Strawberry Pudding which conjures up wonderful memories of Grandmother's house and many special family dinners.

1 box vanilla wafers
1 cup sugar
3 tablespoons flour
3 eggs, separated (add a pinch salt to egg whites which will be whipped for topping)
1 teaspoon vanilla
3 tablespoons butter
2 boxes frozen presweetened sliced strawberries thawed
2 cups sweet milk

meringue
½ cup sugar
¼ teaspoon cream of tartar
reserved egg whites

Preheat oven to 400 degrees • Beat egg yolks in mixing bowl and set aside • Mix sugar and flour in sauce pan • Add milk, vanilla and butter, cook over low heat • Mix one or two spoonfuls of warm milk mixture to eggs yolks to keep from curdling • Slowly add well beaten egg yolks to mixture in saucepan • Stir constantly until mixture begins to thicken and becomes the consistency of pudding • In a two quart baking dish, line bottom and sides with wafers • Alternately add strawberries and wafers, with top layer being wafers • Pour pudding mixture over the layered strawberries and wafers •

Stan and MaMa

∼ᴐ continued ᴐ∼

Beat egg whites with ½ cup
sugar and ¼ teaspoon cream of
tartar until stiff • Spread over
pudding • Bake at 400 degrees
for 6-8 minutes or until brown •
Allow to cool before serving

banana pudding

3 ¼ cups milk
½ cup sugar
1 teaspoon vanilla extract
3 eggs, separated (reserve
  2 of the egg whites for
  meringue)
4 teaspoons flour
4 bananas, sliced

meringue
2 egg whites (reserved)
½ cup sugar
½ teaspoon vanilla extract

I can still feel the excitement and smell the food at the all day singings and homecomings with dinner on the ground at Stateline Freewill Baptist Church in Elkwood, AL. There was no fellowship hall – just make-shift wooden tables made with boards on sawhorses on the lawn. The country air became a smorgasbord of aromas: fried chicken, chicken and dumplings, corn on the cob, ham that had never seen a processing plant except the inside of a smokehouse!

But best of all, I remember person after person asking my mom, "Mrs. Wilburn, did you bring banana pudding?" And she did – always.

When you follow this recipe, you'll have every ingredient except one. Mom always put in lots of love, and that makes it twice as good!

In a large bowl, mix 3 cups milk with ½ cup sugar and 1 teaspoon vanilla extract; set aside • Beat 3 egg yolks until stiff and slowly add to milk mixture • In a separate bowl, add flour to remaining ¼ cup milk, and mix until smooth; set aside • In a saucepan cook the egg and milk mixture on medium heat, stirring constantly until it thickens • Continue stirring, adding flour mixture until it thickens to the consistency of pudding • Line an 8 x 11 inch glass baking dish with vanilla wafers • Add a layer of banana slices, then repeat with one more layer each of wafers and bananas • Pour pudding over the four layers and top with meringue (below)

meringue
Preheat oven to 400 degrees •
In a mixing bowl, beat 2 reserved egg whites until stiff, gradually add sugar and vanilla • Gently scrape bowl and pour meringue over pudding mixture • Bake at 400 degrees for 6-8 minutes or until lightly browned

AARON WILBURN

Aaron with his mom

Down a side road in Dunnville, KY, stands a little, square, white house with a tin roof. It is where my grandmother and grandfather lived and raised a family. It is where my mother and her five siblings were born. It is also the site of some of the most precious memories of my childhood. My granny made the best biscuits this seven-year-old boy had ever tasted. They melted in my mouth. She canned vegetables and preserves. She could cook up anything in no time flat. She was equipped with a standard pressure cooker, cast iron skillets, bucket of lard, bright floral wallpaper and a funeral home fan for those hot days in July.

Her tiny kitchen was always crowded on holidays when my aunts and cousins all got together to cook. They would sample and stir, sample and stir and whisper when seven-year-old boys walked into the room. The aroma I can remember to this day was from a hot pan of buttermilk cornbread coming out of the oven.

This recipe for cornbread dressing has been in my family for at least 50 years. It started with Granny. Then my mother, in a risky experiment, decided to add a can of cream of mushroom soup to the mix.

That "secret" ingredient has made her cornbread dressing a hit every time it has been served. It has remained a secret until this book. My cousins will be shocked to know that a mere can of soup made my mom's dish the main attraction.

Now, my wife and daughters make the dressing together. And I, well, I do my part to make sure it doesn't last very long.

KEVIN WILLIAMS

Granny and Kevin

granny's dressing

dressing
prepared cornbread
½ stick butter
1 onion, chopped
3 ¼ cups chicken broth,
  reserve 2 cups for gravy
1 (8 ounces) can cream of
  mushroom soup
1 teaspoon sage

gravy
2 cups reserved broth
½ cup cold water
2 tablespoons cornstarch

Make one batch of your favorite cornbread (9 x 9 inch or 8 x 8 inch pan) – it tastes best in a cast iron skillet • After it has cooled, crumble into a large mixing bowl • Preheat oven to 400 degrees • Grease cookie sheet • Melt ½ stick of butter in a small skillet or sauce pan • Add ¾ cup of finely chopped onions and sauté until soft • Pour onions over the cornbread • Add 1 ¼ cups of chicken broth and stir • Add one can cream of mushroom soup and stir again • Sprinkle in sage and mix well • Scoop dressing mixture with an ice cream scoop into a ball and drop onto prepared cookie sheet about 2 inches apart • Sprinkle tops with paprika • Bake at 400 degrees for 40-45 minutes until they are crispy on the edges

For the gravy, heat 2 cups of chicken broth on high until it starts to boil • Reduce heat • Whisk together ½ cup cold water with 2 tablespoons cornstarch • Stir cornstarch mixture into broth • Stir occasionally on medium heat for 2-3 minutes until slightly thickened • Serve gravy separately as an optional topping for the dressing

gerald's famous cheese toast

For years, Houston's Restaurant was a Nashville favorite. It was also a favorite for Greater Vision's Gerald Wolfe and George Younce. Well, until the restaurant took their favorite appetizer off the menu – cheese toast. Suffering from withdrawal, Younce and Wolfe were willing to do anything to have that cheese toast in all its greasy, gourmet goodness back on their plates. So, they took matters into their own hands. "George and I set out to see if we could duplicate that recipe," remembers Gerald.

They took to their respective kitchens, hoping that one or the other would ultimately recreate the beloved Houston's cheese toast. "I'm always experimenting with stuff like that," Wolfe says. It took Wolfe about two weeks, but he nailed it.

Since then, anyone privileged enough to set foot in Wolfe's kitchen has been treated to the famous crunchy treat. And Wolfe says it's so good, "they pass out." Although Wolfe painstakingly developed his own recipe, he agreed to share it. However, it comes with no guarantees that your batch will match his!

1 loaf egg bread or italian bread
1 pound mild cheddar cheese, grated
1 pound monterey jack cheese, grated
¾ stick butter
parmesan cheese to taste

Preheat oven to 350 degrees • Melt butter in saucepan or microwave • Slice bread to one inch thick slices • Place bread slices on cookie sheet • Spread melted butter over the bread liberally • Spread grated cheeses over the bread liberally • Finally, sprinkle with parmesan cheese • Bake 5-8 minutes or until cheese is fully melted, being careful not to brown

GERALD WOLFE

Greater Vision:
Rodney Griffin,
Gerald Wolfe and
Jason Waldroup

maria's mexican eggs

Vonnie's mom, Maria, lives with us now, and Maria wanted to add her family's favorite breakfast dish to the mix. What a blessing it is for Vonnie and me to watch both of our mothers, who worked hard and gave so much of their lives to raise their kids, smile and enjoy preparing these wonderful foods for the hungry mouths of their grown children. Though the kids have grown up and changed, the tastes, smells and the LOVE are exactly the same!!!!!

1 dozen eggs, whisked
1 large onion, diced
4 tomatoes, diced
¾ of a 16 ounce jar mild banana peppers, drained and reserve liquid
1 pound of bacon, chopped

Fry chopped bacon pieces in a large skillet until crisp • Remove bacon and ¾ of bacon grease from skillet • Add chopped onion to remaining grease and sauté until brown and tender • Add peppers and ¼ of reserved pepper juice to onions and cook for approximately 10 minutes • Add tomatoes and cook for 5 minutes • Add eggs to skillet, stirring gently until eggs are set • Bacon pieces can be stirred into eggs or sprinkled on top • Serve hot

WOODY WRIGHT

Vonnie and her mother, Maria

betty's chocolate syrup and biscuits

My mother, Betty, and my brothers, Michael and David, recently came to visit Vonnie and me at our home. This special occasion called for our family's favorite breakfast food - Chocolate Syrup and Biscuits. My late father's family loved this combination and so did my mother's family. It is a depression era breakfast that has stood the test of time in our family. No family breakfast is complete without this simple, yummy dish.

chocolate syrup
2 tablespoons cocoa
1 ½ cups sugar
1 ½ cups water

biscuits
4 cups self-rising flour
½ cup shortening
½ cup buttermilk

Preheat oven to 450 degrees • Grease cookie sheet • In a large bowl, combine flour and shortening and work together by hand • Add buttermilk to thicken dough and again mix by hand • Flatten mixture onto floured wax paper and lightly sprinkle the top of dough with flour • Cut out biscuits using medium sized drinking glass • Place biscuits on prepared cookie sheet and bake at 450 degrees for 12-15 minutes or until golden brown • Remove biscuits from oven and let cool • Top with chocolate gravy

While biscuits bake, combine cocoa, sugar and water in a large saucepan and bring to a boil, stirring constantly • Reduce heat and allow to thicken

Woody and his mother, Betty

WOODY WRIGHT

mamma tom's cream gravy

¼ cup bacon or sausage grease
½ cup flour
1 (12 ounce) can evaporated milk
1 can water

Heat bacon or sausage grease on medium to high heat in a 10 inch iron skillet • When grease becomes hot, stir in ½ cup of flour and continue stirring until it thickens to a paste and becomes brown – the browner, the better • Add one can of evaporated milk and one can of water • Continue stirring to prevent sticking and cook until it becomes thick and comes to a boil • Pour gravy into a bowl • Serve over biscuits, eggs, chicken, mashed potatoes, rice, etc.

I'll always remember as a young boy waking up to the familiar smell of bacon grease and flour browning in an old iron skillet. And when Mamma would open up our wood stove, the smell of homemade biscuits would bring me out of bed on the coldest of mornings. I'd grab my clothes and run to the fireplace where I had left my shoes on the hearth so they'd be nice and warm to slip into. I'd then run to the kitchen table where everything was waiting for me. I could help myself to whatever I wanted and eat to my heart and belly's content! There was never a morning that my breakfast wasn't waiting for me, never a morning that I didn't wake up to those familiar smells and comforting sounds of Mamma in the kitchen. It was a constant in my life, and as simple as it was, it meant the world to this little boy.

I may not have the privilege of waking up to Mamma's biscuits and gravy anymore, but I thank God that I had a mamma and daddy who loved me unconditionally and taught me that Jesus does, too. I now wake up every morning with the comfort of knowing that Jesus loves me, He died for me, and He will always be there for me. He is my constant, and He means the world to this "little boy."

Submitted by George Younce before his death in 2005

GEORGE YOUNCE

George with parents, Tom and Nellie

Gloria and her mother, Dorothy Sickal, with
daughters, Suzanne and Amy, at Gaither's Pond

Old friends having fun in Bill's old convertible:
Hovie Lister, Jake Hess, Rex Nelon, J.D. Sumner,
Bill Gaither, Jessy Dixon and Jack Toney

index

Name	Recipe	Page

recipe notes

recipe notes

recipe notes

recipe notes

recipe notes

recipe notes

recipe notes

recipe notes

recipe notes